PRACTICAL

FENG SHUI
ASTROLOGY

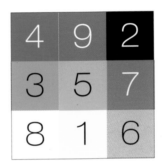

SIMON BROWN

WARD LOCK

I dedicate this book to my father Michael Brown and grandmothers Marjory Knox and Louise Brown

A WARD LOCK BOOK
This edition was published in the United Kingdom by
Ward Lock
Wellington House
125 Strand
London WC2R OBB

A Cassell imprint

First published 1999

Created and produced by
CARROLL & BROWN LIMITED
20 Lonsdale Road
London NW6 6RD

Project Editor Madeleine Jennings

Senior Designer Evie Loizides
Designers Kenta Namba, Sandra Brooke

Managing Editor Rachel Aris
Managing Art Editor Tracy Timson

British Library Catalogue-in-Publication Data
A catalogue record for this book is available from the British Library

ISBN 0-7063-7825-3

Reproduced by Colourscan, Singapore
Printed and bound in Great Britain by Bath Press Group

Contents

what is feng shui astrology?

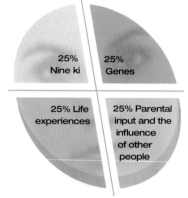

25% Nine ki	25% Genes
25% Life experiences	25% Parental input and the influence of other people

The influence of nine ki
Different factors influence a person's character to greater and lesser degrees. Your genes, upbringing and life experience all play a part, together with the impact of nine ki energy. If these influences were equal, the proportions would be the same as the chart above.

The Japanese system of feng shui astrology, also known as nine ki astrology, is one of the oldest forms of astrology in the world. It is based on the principle that there is a constantly moving energy force, known as ki, that pervades the universe. At the moment you were born, the most influential planets were in certain positions in space, which created a particular pattern of energy flow that helped to shape your character. In the years following your birth there has been a series of other energy patterns, and your own personal energy has mixed and continues to mix with these. What these energies are, how time and direction affect them, and how they affect you, your behaviour and your relationships with others, are covered in this book.

Using feng shui astrology

An understanding of feng shui astrology will help you to better connect with the forces of nature or ki energy, which can work for you or against you. It can provide invaluable information on aspects of your character and your potential reactions in different circumstances. It can also help you to analyse others. Bear in mind, though, that people are individual and there are many factors other than ki energy that influence personality and behaviour. Yet if feng shui astrology enables you to gain even a small insight into your or another person's character, you will be at a considerable advantage in the world. Feng shui astrology can make a positive contribution to the following areas of your life.

Family You can put your knowledge of ki energy into practice to help you decide on the best time to conceive. Or, if you are having problems conceiving, it may be reassuring to find out that you are coming into a particularly favourable time. Later, you will be able to use feng shui astrology to better understand your children's feelings and behaviour.

Moving When you move, you take yourself out of one kind of ki energy and replant yourself into another, which can have a profound effect on your life. It is therefore important to try to move in a direction that takes you into a ki energy that will help you in whatever you are trying to do in life. Each year a different ki energy will take up its position in a specific direction. You can then either work out which directions are best for you in a particular year or which year will be best for you to move in a particular direction.

Relationships Feng shui astrology can not only help you better understand another person, it can also show you how compatible your two ki energies are. You can use it to identify the areas in which you work well together, as well as to highlight areas of potential conflict and find ways of preventing problems. It can also help you decide when to start a relationship, get engaged or married and assist you in helping children and work-mates achieve their full potentials.

Career Feng shui astrology will help you understand the type of career in which you are most likely to succeed. It will also help you to work out the best time to make important decisions and changes, or take new initiatives. Certain times are more practical than others to start a new career, achieve greater recognition, ask for a raise, take on a leadership position or, eventually, retire – this book will help you identify these times.

Business If you are thinking of starting your own business, you can use feng shui astrology to help you plan ahead. The best time to start a business; how to build a well-balanced team; when to expand, be more competitive or focus on team building; a good moment to enter new markets, try to win awards or increase sales; when to hold PR events; at what point to float on the stock market, arrange loans or sell the business; when to develop internal systems or concentrate on customer relations – all these can be ascertained using feng shui astrology. You can also use it to assess when and where to set up subsidiary companies or relocate.

Travel Most times you travel you will have the opportunity to choose the best day and month to do so. This is essential if the trip is important in terms of business or family needs, such as going to sign contracts, purchasing a new property, meeting your parents-in-law for the first time, giving an important sales talk, attending an interview, giving a lecture or planning to propose marriage. Ideally, you would always be able to travel in favourable directions; however, in real life this is not always easy to achieve. If you travel frequently, you should try to use feng shui astrology so that you travel in a favourable direction more often than you did so before, and that you avoid the directions that are potentially most harmful.

Principles of feng shui astrology

part one

Feng shui astrology can help you work out how to be in the right place at the right time and therefore make the most of opportunities. To learn how to do this, however, you first need to understand the basic concepts of feng shui astrology. These consist of ki energy, yin and yang, the five elements, the eight directions and the magic square.

ki energy

n many parts of the world people believe that there is an invisible energy that flows throughout the universe: through your body, the food you eat, your home and workplace, and the air that surrounds you. This energy is known as *ki* in Japan, *chi* in China and *prana* in India. In this book I will refer to it as ki energy because the particular form of feng shui astrology I use is predominantly practised in Japan.

Like other forces of nature, ki energy is not static. It travels from one person or entity to another through solid matter and through space. This constant movement means that your personal energy is continuously intermingling with the ki around you. The premise underlying feng shui astrology is that by understanding the movement of ki energy through space – that is, in your surroundings – you can time your behaviour in such a way that the ambient ki mixes compatibly with your personal ki energy to promote your health and happiness.

To understand the flow of ki energy, we have to examine how it moves through the universe. Just as the earth sends ripples of ki energy spiralling out into space, the planets surrounding the earth are also absorbing, processing and radiating ki energy. As the earth revolves around the sun, its position relative to the other planets changes, causing the ki energy from these planets to mix with the earth's ki energy in different ways every day. Because the movement of the planets is cyclical, so too is the flow of ki, following a nine-year cycle (and within that, monthly, daily and even hourly cycles: see also page 108).

According to feng shui astrology, there are nine types of ki energy, each associated with a particular year, month, day and hour. The type of energy prevalent when you were born shapes your character, the way you do things and how you lead your life. It also influences how you relate to other types of ki energy. With the aid of your own personal feng shui birth chart (based on the energy prevalent when you were were born: see pages 34–73), feng shui astrology can help you understand the nature of the nine different types of ki energies and how they affect you, enabling you to formulate a strategy that will bring you success in life.

Each year the prevailing ki energy changes and influences your own ki energy in a different way, determining whether it is a good or bad time for you to do embark on a new endeavour. If you use the energy to your advantage you will find that it is easier to achieve certain things, rather like swimming with the tide rather than against it. Feng shui astrology can provide you with essential clues as to when to make important changes or decisions in your life, for example, when to begin a new job, get married or move house. It's biggest influence is on the timing of events.

It is often said that to be successful in life all you need is to be in the right place at the right time and have one good contact and luck. By learning how to read your birth chart (see pages 34–73) you can learn how to be in the right place at the right time and make that precious bit of luck for yourself!

Energy points in your body

Ki energy flows throughout your body, but it is concentrated in seven key areas that are known as chakras. These seven chakras are situated at the crown of your head, between your eyes, at your throat, your heart, solar plexus, just below your navel and at your coccyx.

Personal ki energy

Your date of birth, rather than that of your conception, is used to determine your personal ki energy. This is because you were submerged in your mother's ki energy until you were born.

yin and yang

These two Oriental words are used to describe the opposite yet complementary nature of the ki energy flowing through the universe. Broadly speaking, yin describes a more passive kind of energy, while yang is active. Yin and yang relate to everything in the universe, so you and your surroundings are made up of a combination of these two qualities – some things being more yin, others being more yang. This is as true for your physical, emotional and mental states as it is for the food you eat, the buildings you live and work in, the activities you pursue and the lifestyles you create for yourself. Indeed, practitioners of Chinese medicine base their diagnoses on the concepts of yin and yang. For example, if a person complained of being weak, lethargic or depressed, he or she is likely to be too yin. To address this imbalance, treatment would involve 'taking in more yang' by eating more yang foods (warming, strengthening foods such as hearty soups and thick stews), taking more dynamic yang exercise and following a structured, routine lifestyle to reach a more healthy balanced state.

The concepts of yin and yang help to explain the cycles of ki energy change that we all experience. Because ki energy changes constantly, it is more yin or more yang at different times of the day, at different points within the lunar cycle and in different seasons. Therefore, by understanding how ki changes over time you can work with the prevailing ki energy, both to plan ahead better and to address any problem areas in your life.

Energy changes during the day

Yin and yang change throughout the day; for example, midday has the most yang atmosphere whereas midnight is most yin. At night ki energy is more yin, which is ideal for sleep (although some people are at their most creative during the night and find it a particularly good time to write poetry or music, or think of ideas for a novel). It is also a time when you might find it easier to look deep inside yourself for answers about your life. As the night wears on, the ki energy

A balanced partnership

Yin and yang personalities, such as Laurel and Hardy, tend make great partners, both professional and personal.

becomes less yin. As the sun comes up over the horizon, a strong yang ki energy is introduced, which is associated with getting up, starting a new day and being active. Throughout the morning the ki becomes increasingly yang, making the early part of the day a good time for more yang activities, such as exercising, getting work done, being focussed, and concentrating on or starting new projects. At midday the environmental ki energy reaches its most yang. However, ki energy quickly changes to becoming more yin as the sun descends in the sky. You can use this more settling ki energy for consolidating your morning's efforts, being practical and achieving greater realism. The powerful ki energy that radiates at sunset is helpful for completing projects, feeling rewarded for your day's work and contemplating the evening's enjoyments.

Energy changes during the lunar cycle

The night is primarily influenced by the moon. Unlike the sun's ki energy, which is more yang, the moon's ki energy is more yin. Within each lunar cycle, the phase of the moon has a strong influence on your behaviour. A full moon, for example, makes your behaviour more yang while a new moon has a more yin effect. Interestingly, it seems that certain events, such as car accidents or pregnant women going into labour, are more likely to happen during and close to a full moon, as they all involve yang behaviour. During the days leading up to a full moon when the energy is predominantly yang, you are likely to feel more active, to want to go out more and be sociable. Therefore, this time of the lunar cycle is perfect for parties, PR events and exhibitions. On the other hand, the days preceding a new moon are advantageous for more yin activities including healing, therapy and meditation.

Energy changes from season to season

Yin and yang also vary with the seasons, the winter being the most yin and the summer the most yang. The yin energy of autumn and winter is good for consolidating gains, being practical and completing projects, while the more yang spring and summer are good times to explore new avenues, be active and become more ambitious. Furthermore, someone born in the winter will be more yang in character than someone born in the summer, because the mother will have eaten a more warming yang diet during her pregnancy, making her baby more yang.

Geographical influences

The concepts of yin and yang can be applied to geographical locations. Someone who is born and lives in a colder climate is going to be more yang than someone who comes from a hot climate. This is because children brought up in colder areas eat more warming yang foods, such as porridge, stews, casseroles and thick soups, whereas those who grow up in hot climates will eat more cooling yin foods, such as salads, fruits and juices.

the five elements

4 Tree	**9** Fire	**2** Soil
3 Tree	**5** Soil	**7** Metal
8 Soil	**1** Water	**6** Metal

Which element are you?

To identify your element, work out your code of numbers (see pages 15 or 20). The element associated with each number is given above.

According to feng shui astrology, there are five fundamental life forces or elements: soil, tree, fire, metal and water. Everything in the universe – the seasons, colours, your character and even parts of the body – can be classified as one of these five elements. What's more, each of the nine different types of ki energy is associated with one of the five elements. One of the fundamental principles of feng shui astrology is the way in which the five elements interact with each other. Each person has features of a particular element, so by understanding which elements are supportive or destructive of each other, you can predict how people with different ki energies will behave together.

The illustration opposite shows the way each element relates to the others. The flow of ki energy from one element to the next in a clockwise direction is known as the support cycle. Each element supports the next and is calmed or, in more extreme circumstances, drained in the process. For example, someone with fire energy will 'support' someone with soil energy but is also liable to be drained by the relationship. The star-shaped lines inside show what is called the

Relationship compatibility based on the five elements

Water – Water These two partners will identify with each other, but should respect each other's desire to spend time alone. This could mean seeing little of each other for periods of time.

Water – Tree This is a harmonious relationship where the person with water ki energy is independent and supportive to the person with tree ki energy, who is busy and career orientated.

Water – Fire The fire ki energy person may feel thwarted while the water ki energy person may be overwhelmed. Doing things together will help introduce more tree ki energy, which makes for a more harmonious relationship.

Water – Soil The soil ki energy person is more dependent, cautious and careful, and may stifle the water ki energy person's independent spirit.

Metal ki energy in the form of material wealth would make this combination more harmonious.

Water – Metal This is potentially harmonious. Metal ki energy people enjoy love and affection, and water ki energy people are naturally affectionate. However, they need to be generous with their affection to keep the relationship alive.

Tree – Tree This relationship is based on good understanding and both partners are able to actively pursue their careers. However, being more of a career-orientated relationship, it may lack passion, intimacy and affection.

Tree – Fire The tree ki energy person provides support and stimulation, while the fire ki energy person organises the couple's active outgoing lifestyle that they both enjoy.

destructive cycle, which applies to two ki energies that are not next to each other. For example, in a relationship involving soil and water ki energies, the couple would be embroiled in a turbulent situation where one partner could control, stifle or frustrate the other. Although such partners would need to compromise more and be able to accept each other's differences to find harmony, they do have the advantage of a more exciting relationship and the benefit of being able to take the other into experiences he or she may not normally try.

In a group of people, such as a work team or a traditional extended-family household (in which parents, children, grandparents and sometimes unmarried aunts all live together), there is likely to be a healthy mix of all the five element ki energies, thereby increasing the potential for harmony. It can be harder for just two people living together to achieve a long-term harmonious relationship unless they have particularly compatible five element ki energies. The chances of success are good for two people of the same five element ki energy as they likely to be able to understand each other better, but there is a risk that the relationship could stagnate.

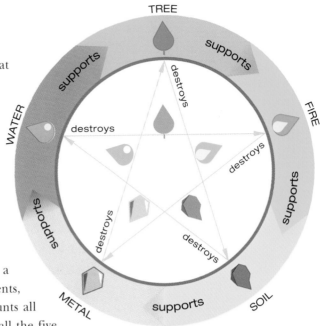

Supportive or destructive?

Each element in the cycle has a supportive relationship with the element on either side, but is disharmonious with the other two.

Tree – Soil The person with tree ki energy may overwhelm the soil ki energy person and become impatient with their slow, more cautious approach. An active social life is the key to greater harmony.

Tree – Metal A metal ki energy person can be too organised for the more reckless style of a tree ki energy person. A more sexual relationship creates more water ki energy, which is harmonious with both tree and metal ki people.

Fire – Fire An emotional and passionate relationship. Upsets can cause frequent separations, although the two tend to be reunited.

Fire – Soil This is a harmonious relationship with the soil ki energy person calming the more emotional side of the fire ki energy person. Both partners share a caring approach to relationships.

Fire – Metal The more passionate and spontaneous fire ki energy person may find the metal ki energy person too organised and reserved. More soil ki energy in the form of building a home together will help.

Soil – Soil Both partners share many values in life and also understand each other well, but may get bored with one another and feel the need to seek out more exciting company.

Soil – Metal This is a harmonious relationship where both like to take a long-term approach to life, growing closer together.

Metal – Metal This can be harmonious with mutual interest in wealth, style and having fun. Keeping partner options open, however, can make this a less secure relationship.

the eight directions

The eight directions

The feng shui compass I use divides the circle into unequal segments as shown. The north is always at the bottom, which is the traditional style of Oriental maps.

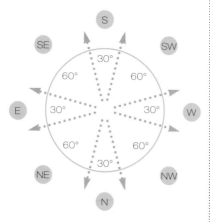

Moving to a new home

The timing and direction of a move affects your compatibility with the new ki energy (see pages 107–25).

Another aspect to feng shui astrology is understanding the concept of eight directions, which is the basis of the compass style of feng shui. This further refinement of ki energy relates to space and location. (The compass used in feng shui is divided into segments of 30° and 60°. The 30° segments are 15° either side of due north, east, south and west, while the 60° segments are 30° either side of due north-east, south-east, south-west and north-west: see left.) Each of the eight directions is associated with a different kind of ki energy, and therefore has implications for your personal achievements.

Every year your personal ki mixes best with ki energies found in one or more of the eight directions. Because the pattern of ki changes year by year, the directions that are favourable or unfavourable also change. When choosing the best time to make an important decision, you can combine your knowledge about when it would be propitious for an event to occur with the prevailing direction's influences. In this way, you can decide not only *when* to start a new job, for instance, but *where* best to focus your energies in the search for that job. You can also use an understanding of the ki energy of the eight directions in a wider geographical context, for example when planning long-distance travel.

The concept of the eight directions has implications for more than just travel or moves: it can help you make personal decisions about your life or find possible ways of resolving problem areas. For example, if you have been experiencing difficulties in conceiving and are thinking of moving house, you could consider moving north, as this direction is associated in feng shui astrology with conception. If you are not planning a move, you could try instead to focus your energies on the northern part of your home – perhaps by redecorating, spring cleaning or putting some new plants here.

Certain endeavours are associated with each direction – the south-east, for example, is linked with creativity while the west is associated with romance. When trying to achieve a particular goal, turn to the chart on page 122 to identify the appropriate direction; you could then try to sleep with the top of your head pointing in that direction, which may bring success more easily.

Each direction is linked not only to one of the nine different types of ki energy, but also to one of the five elements, as well as to a particular time and season, during which the ki energy of that direction will be most active (see pages 74–93).

the magic square

As you can see by now, there are many different aspects of feng shui astrology – but the magic square links these all together. The magic square is said to have had its origins in northern China where, in about 4000 BC, a man named Fu Hsi had become well known for building up the banks of the River Lo to prevent the flooding that had been a regular occurrence. One day, as Fu Hsi was meditating on the banks of the river, he noticed a tortoise crawl out of the water. On its back he saw a remarkable pattern of water drops that he was very struck by. The tortoise's shell was shaped in a rough square, divided into nine compartments, and each compartment contained a group of droplets making a different number between one and nine. What makes the square a magic one is that the numbers are arranged in such a way that each line of numbers always adds up to fifteen, whether they are combined horizontally, vertically or diagonally (see illustration right).

Fu Hsi later gathered together many scholars to try to create a single elegant system that took account of all the various prevailing philosophies. To this end, each of the nine numbers in the magic square was given a description in terms of yin and yang, was related to one of the five elements (water, tree, fire, soil and metal) and one of the eight directions. As a result, each number has a complete character that describes its particular type of ki energy. By bringing all this knowledge together, Fu Hsi helped to create a powerful tool, which was then used to understand the universe and everything within it. You, too, can access this power by using feng shui astrology to direct your life.

According to feng shui astrology, you can use the magic square, which functions as both a map and a timetable, to chart the movements of your ki energy for each year, month, day and hour, so that you can calculate what to do and when (the year having the greatest influence and the hour the smallest). Each of the nine numbers of the magic square is associated with a particular kind of ki energy. The arrangement of the numbers represents the prevailing pattern of ki energy in each of the nine years in the cycle (see pages 118–125); the pattern changes each year and so is represented by a different chart. The nine numbers of the magic square are associated with nine of the most influential stars and planets – the sun, the moon, Venus, Jupiter, Saturn, Mars, Neptune, Uranus and Pluto. The various alignments of these heavenly bodies are meant to be reflected in the nine different patterns of the nine ki numbers (see pages 118–25).

Fu Hsi's tortoise

You can use the magic square to work out the predominant energy when you were born, which enables you to make the important decisions in your life.

Your code of nine ki numbers

The three numbers that make up your individual code are calculated from your year of birth, month of birth and a combination of these two numbers. Each number gives a basic assessment of specific aspects of your character and provides insights into your most successful strategy in life. To find your full code of numbers at a glance, see page 20.

your nine ki year number

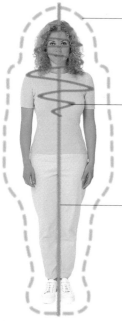

the axis number relates to the ki energy around the surface of the body

the month number relates to the ki energy of the mind, emotions and upper body

the year number relates to the ki energy of the central spiritual channel

As well as defining your underlying character, your nine ki year number also represents your basic values and deepest nature. Someone with the nine ki year number eight, for example, will always have a deeply competitive nature, whereas someone with a nine ki year number six will value honesty, dignity and respect. These basic values stay with a person from birth to old age.

Knowing the qualities of your nine ki year number will also provide essential information on how you will progress in life (see the chart opposite). This information is particularly useful when developing a long-term strategy. If you have the nine ki year number one, for example, you would be best advised to build up your career slowly. As water is the element associated with number one, it's easy to compare this strategy to a small brook growing slowly but steadily into a powerful river. People with the year number one should not worry if a friend with a year number three seems to be rushing ahead in life and reaching greater heights. Later on in life, when the person with year number three is flagging, you could steadily be increasing your power.

year number attributes

	MOST SUCCESSFUL STRATEGY FOR LIFE	CAREER QUALITIES/CHOICES	DEEPEST NATURE
1	Slowly developing Increasing power Flexibility	Artistic/ Medicines Healing	Reserved Secretive Spiritual
2	Being steady Exercising care Consistency Improving quality	Home based Family based/ Food industry Working with people Care giver	Practical Dependent Family orientated Motherly Caring
3	Getting off to a quick start Pushing forwards Making things happen	Accurate At the forefront/ Science Design Progressive arts	Ambitious Progressive Enthusiastic Active Dynamic
4	Being harmonious Taking a progressive approach Forward planning	Creative/ Media Travel Distribution Communication	Creative Sensitive Persistent Unexpectedly strong Determined
5	Being changeable Attracting opportunities Having periods of calm	A centre of attention A prime mover/ Politics Food industry Business	Powerful Tending to extremes Opinionated Highly moral Prone to stagnation
6	Making long-term plans Tackling tasks in a methodical way Being steady going	Intuitive/ Management Administration Leadership Self employment	Dignified Trustworthy Scrupulous Responsible Respectable
7	A positive outlook Working towards outcomes Being motivated by wealth	Thorough/ Finance Entertainment Business	Pleasure seeking Youthful Playful Stylish Charming
8	Seeking new opportunities Making sudden changes Moving quickly	Competitive Speculative/ Property Trading Investments	Hard working Self motivated Outgoing Playful
9	Being emotionally led Having bursts of energy Social networking	Sociable/ Sales Public recognition Future trends	Passionate Proud Noticeable Quick

Calculating your year number

You can determine your year number at a glance by referring to page 20. If you would like to know how to work it out for yourself, however, you need to add the last two digits of your birth year until you get a single digit. For example, if you were born in 1962, then 6+2=8. If you were born in 1969, then 6+9=15, 1+5=6. If you were born between 5 February 1900 and 4 February 2000 (inclusive) subtract this number from 10 to get your year number; for people born after this time subtract from 9. So, someone born in 1969 after 4 February has a year number of four (6+9=15, 1+5=6, 10-6=4). Someone born 4 July 2003 will have a year number of six (0+3=3, 9-3=6). Once you have worked out your nine ki year number, you can study its qualities, which will enable you to put your whole life into perspective.

Unlike the Western calendar, the nine ki year calendar starts on the 3, 4 or 5 of February (the exact dates can be found on the chart on page 20). So if you were born after 31 December and before 3, 4 or 5 of February, your year number will be the same as that for the preceding year. For example, someone born on 10 January 1958 will have seven as his or her year number, which is the year number for 1957. (Please note: the quick reference chart on page 20 has already taken this into account.)

Team players

Your month number indicates the strengths of your character. So, to build a successful team, make sure you have a wide range of month numbers. You can either calculate your month number (see opposite), or simply look it up on page 20.

Conversely, if you have the year number three and you enjoy great success in your early years, it would be wise to find ways to make this last and to save some of your wealth for later years.

Your year number will also help define the choices for a successful, long-term career. We all know that if you can find a career that enables you to harness your natural strengths, your ability to reach the top and to be satisfied is greatly enhanced. If your year number is nine, for example, you will be well suited to a career in sales, PR or advertising. For more information on the qualities of each year number see pages 25–33.

As for relationships, a couple's year numbers are linked to how they will progress in the long term and whether they will tend to grow closer together or further apart. A relationship between a year number six and a year number seven (both numbers with metal energies), for example, will tend to get stronger over the years as both partners share experiences and understand each other. Conversely, a partnership of a year number three and two (tree and soil energies respectively) may become more distant with time as each person drifts towards his or her natural, but different, direction in life. For more information on relationships see pages 94–106.

your nine ki month number

This number relates primarily to the way you think, communicate and feel. In this respect, it has the greatest influence on how you behave on a daily basis and is therefore of primary consideration in terms of romantic relationships.

Your month number will tell how you can best express your ideas and emotions. Moreover, you will be able to improve your understanding of how you communicate with others, which can make or break a relationship, romantic or otherwise. If you have the month number three, for example, you probably tend to be frank and to the point. It is not in your nature to be tactful. A person with the month number four, however, may take this style of communication too personally because he or she is more sensitive. Being aware of and taking into account the nature of people with month number three can thus reduce feelings of hurt.

Let's consider another example of a couple with the month numbers nine and five. In terms of the five elements (see page 10) this relationship is harmonious. However, the individual with the month number five has a powerful, confrontational expression while the person with the month number nine tends to react emotionally and somewhat explosively. Such a relationship can be a recipe for fiery arguments and emotional upsets, especially if the more confrontational person criticises his or her partner. In this situation, each partner needs to find a structured way of communicating when they are upset with the other. It

month number attributes

	THINKING	COMMUNICATION	EMOTIONS
1	Objective Independent Rational	Fluid Open Natural	Deep Emotional Hidden
2	Methodical Practical Realistic	Careful Tactful Understandable	Caring Dependent Kind
3	Focused Precise Futuristic	Frank To the point Assertive	Confident Highly strung Enthusiastic
4	Imaginative Creative Original	Persuasive Persistent Non-confrontational	Gentle Sensitive Romantic
5	Black and white Centred Functional	Powerful Understated Seductive	Changeable Determined Attention seeking
6	Organised Intuitive Decisive	Honest Cautious Respectful	Controlled Dignified Restrained
7	Goal orientated Positive Stylish	Charming Entertaining Playful	Fun-loving Reflective Depressive
8	Competitive Quick Clever	Clear Convincing Pushy	Alert Fragile Quick to change
9	Fast Sharp Spontaneous	Passionate Expressive Flamboyant	Fiery Impulsive Proud

Calculating your month number

1	4	7	8 (soil)
2	5	8	2 (soil)
3	6	9	5 (soil)

You can either look up your month number on page 20, or calculate it as follows. Every February and November starts with a soil number. To identify the soil number for the February or November of your birth year, find your year number in the matrix above, then look along the row to the soil number (in the last column). The month number decreases by one each month, so if February is a 2 month, March will be a 1 month, April is a 9 month (as the cycle starts again) and so on. Someone born on 21 July 1953, for example, has a year number 2 and a month number 6. Nine ki months start between the 3rd and 9th day of Western calendar months. If you were born before the 3rd day of any month, refer to the preceding month. To find the exact start date of any month, see page 20.

Working well together

Your axis number determines how you are likely to work and interact socially. This can be useful for establishing relationships, whether social or professional.

might be sensible, for instance, if neither responds to any criticism until the following day; in this type of relationship accusations should never be made in the heat of the moment.

Another important factor that can determine the success of a relationship is the way in which people connect emotionally. When this connection is mutual it can lead to a deeper, more satisfying relationship. When people are not emotionally compatible, they can feel misunderstood, which can lead to a situation where every little upset creates a deeper rift. Everyone can experience all different kinds of emotions, although some will be felt more powerfully than others. The emotions associated with your month number will tend to affect you more deeply and more frequently. Use the chart on the previous page to discover your strongest emotional traits and compare these with someone you are close to. This is most applicable in romantic or family relationships. Consider a brother and sister with the month numbers six and seven respectively, for example. The brother, with the month number six, will probably endeavour to be a dignified, responsible, authoritative and self-controlled individual, while his sister, with the month number seven will be more playful, seek pleasures, enjoy teasing and have fun. The sister might thus find her brother too serious, responsible and formal; conversely, the brother will find it hard to join in with his sister in terms of letting go and having fun. Pages 25–33 provide more information on the attributes of each number.

your nine ki axis number

The last number in your code is a calculation of your year and month number and is called the nine ki axis number. It relates to your most superficial ki energy and often influences someone's first impression of you. This ki energy also illustrates how you do things, which is useful in assessing how you work professionally.

Many people may know you according to your more superficial axis ki energy because this is what first stands out about someone when you meet them. You then begin to relate to other people in terms of their month energies; it is only when you get to know someone much better that you can appreciate each other in terms of your deeper year energies. Because the year energy may be very different to your other energies, people may be surprised to know the deeper you. People who have the year number eight, the month number three and the axis number one (code 831), for example, can appear quiet and easy going on the surface. Deep down, however, they are active and dynamic. In contrast, people with the same axis and year numbers will be intrinsically the same as you first perceive them. If you have the year seven, the month five and the axis seven (code 757) you will be playful both on the surface and deep down.

Some combinations can cause confusion. A 766, for example, will seem serious on the surface, and as you get to know him or her in terms of the month number, this person will still seem dignified, responsible and organised. It is only when you really get to know the person well that he or she will reveal their more playful, fun-loving side. Sometimes, due to upbringing and life experiences, a person may have suppressed this side altogether.

If your axis number is different from your deeper energies, you can switch into being a different person at work than at home. A 748 can be shrewd, competitive and motivated at work but gentle, vivacious and amusing in a more relaxed environment. The chart on the right provides you with examples of how people with each axis number may appear professionally.

The numbers in your code that relate to different kinds of ki energy also indicate that you can go through quick changes of personality. For example, if your code is 196, you have water, fire and metal energies. You enjoy solitude, but at other times are sociable, passionate and fiery, and at work you are highly organised. Although this provides variety, you may seem inconsistent to others. Someone with a nine ki code that has similar energies, such as 225 (all soil ki energies), will seem more consistent in all his or her characteristics, regardless of any changes in circumstances. For more details please refer to pages 25–33.

axis number attributes

	FIRST IMPRESSION	WORK
1	Laid back Easy going Flexible	Objective Independent Artistic
2	Social Friendly Considerate	Thorough Cooperative Careful
3	Direct Knowledgeable Solution orientated	Accurate Enthusiastic Technical
4	Gentle Kind Interesting	Creative Full of ideas Determined
5	Tough Confrontational Potentially intimidating	Influential Opinionated Noticeable
6	Correct Formal Opinionated	Well organised Forward thinking Serious
7	Charming Stylish Charismatic	Goal orientated Financially motivated Light hearted
8	Direct Inquisitive Outgoing	Motivated Focused Competitive
9	Social Intelligent Slightly arrogant	Emotional Careful of reputation Good at networking

Calculating your axis number

You can either find your axis number on the chart on page 20, or calculate it as follows. Compare your month number with the number 5. If it is higher than 5, subtract 5 from your month number and then subtract the result from your year number. If your month number is six, for example, and your year number is two, your axis number will be one (6–5=1 and 2–1=1). If your month number is lower than 5, then subtract it from 5 and add the result to your year number. So if your month is four and your year is one, your axis number will be two: 5–4=1 and 1+1=2.

quick reference chart

① **Year**
1937
② Jan 5
③ 00.59
④ Year **1**
⑤ **M6 A9**

How to find your code numbers

First, find your year of birth in the green column (1). Next, look along the row to find the month of your birth (2). If you were born before the particular date and time indicated (2 and 3), you should refer to the previous month. Your year number (4) and your month (M) and axis (A) numbers (5) are then given.

The chart below offers a quick way to identify your year, month and axis numbers; to find out how to use it, see left. The feng shui calendar is slightly different to the Western calendar, which means that the feng shui year begins in February and each month starts at a specific time between the third and ninth day of the Western calendar month. As a result, if you were born in January, your year number will be the same as the previous year. For example, if you were born on 10 January 1954, your year number will be two, whereas anyone born after 4 February 1954 will have the year number one. You should also note the starting date and time for each month, and refer to the previous month if you were born before this time. For example, if you were born before 13.38 on 6 March 1954, your month and axis numbers will be as for February 1954 (M8 A7), and M7 A8 if you were born thereafter. The times in the chart are GMT, so if you were born in a different time zone you will need to add or subtract hours to these times as appropriate.

Year	Jan	Feb	Mar	Apr	May	June	July	Aug	Sept	Oct	Nov	Dec
1937	Jan 5 00.59 Year 1 M6 A9	Feb 4 14:30 Year 9 M5 A9	Mar 6 10:34 Year 9 M4 A1	Apr 4 17:32 Year 9 M3 A2	May 5 13:20 Year 9 M2 A3	June 5 19:34 Year 9 M1 A4	July 7 08:41 Year 9 M9 A5	Aug 7 19:57 Year 9 M8 A6	Sept 8 00:37 Year 9 M7 A7	Oct 8 18:13 Year 9 M6 A8	Nov 7 23.00 Year 9 M5 A9	Dec 7 17.30 Year 9 M4 A1
1938	Jan 6 06:40 Year 9 M3 A2	Feb 4 20:23 Year 8 M2 A2	Mar 6 16:22 Year 8 M1 A3	Apr 4 23:12 Year 8 M9 A4	May 5 18:51 Year 8 M8 A5	June 6 01:01 Year 8 M7 A6	July 7 14:08 Year 8 M6 A7	Aug 8 01:28 Year 8 M5 A8	Sept 8 06:13 Year 8 M4 A9	Oct 8 23:57 Year 8 M3 A1	Nov 8 04:53 Year 8 M2 A2	Dec 7 23:29 Year 8 M1 A3
1939	Jan 6 12:41 Year 8 M9 A4	Feb 5 02:08 Year 7 M8 A4	Mar 6 22:13 Year 7 M7 A5	Apr 5 05:24 Year 7 M6 A6	May 6 00:24 Year 7 M5 A7	June 6 07:39 Year 7 M4 A8	July 7 19:37 Year 7 M3 A9	Aug 8 07:02 Year 7 M2 A1	Sept 8 12:45 Year 7 M1 A2	Oct 9 05:46 Year 7 M9 A3	Nov 8 10:48 Year 7 M8 A4	Dec 8 05:28 Year 7 M7 A5
1940	Jan 6 18:43 Year 7 M6 A6	Feb 5 08:09 Year 6 M5 A6	Mar 6 04:15 Year 6 M4 A7	Apr 4 11:13 Year 6 M3 A8	May 5 07:00 Year 6 M2 A9	June 5 13:15 Year 6 M1 A1	July 7 01:09 Year 6 M9 A2	Aug 7 13:42 Year 6 M8 A3	Sept 7 18:20 Year 6 M7 A4	Oct 8 11:25 Year 6 M6 A5	Nov 7 16:33 Year 6 M5 A6	Dec 7 11:12 Year 6 M4 A7
1941	Jan 6 00:07 Year 6 M3 A8	Feb 4 13:54 Year 5 M2 A8	Mar 6 10:00 Year 5 M1 A9	Apr 4 16:56 Year 5 M9 A1	May 5 12:40 Year 5 M8 A2	June 5 18:52 Year 5 M7 A3	July 7 08:00 Year 5 M6 A4	Aug 7 19:19 Year 5 M5 A5	Sept 8 00:02 Year 5 M4 A6	Oct 8 17:40 Year 5 M3 A7	Nov 7 22:29 Year 5 M2 A8	Dec 6 17:17 Year 5 M1 A9
1942	Jan 6 06:10 Year 5 M9 A1	Feb 4 19:55 Year 4 M8 A1	Mar 6 15:57 Year 4 M7 A2	Apr 4 22:47 Year 4 M6 A3	May 5 18:24 Year 4 M5 A4	June 6 00:29 Year 4 M4 A5	July 7 13:31 Year 4 M3 A6	Aug 8 00:48 Year 4 M2 A7	Sept 8 05:33 Year 4 M1 A8	Oct 8 23:18 Year 4 M9 A9	Nov 8 04:16 Year 4 M8 A1	Dec 7 22:53 Year 4 M7 A2
1943	Jan 6 12:08 Year 4 M6 A3	Feb 5 01:38 Year 3 M5 A3	Mar 6 21:46 Year 3 M4 A4	Apr 5 04:58 Year 3 M3 A5	May 5 23:58 Year 3 M2 A6	June 6 07:08 Year 3 M1 A7	July 7 18:59 Year 3 M9 A8	Aug 8 06:20 Year 3 M8 A9	Sept 8 12:00 Year 3 M7 A1	Oct 9 05:00 Year 3 M6 A2	Nov 8 10:02 Year 3 M5 A3	Dec 8 04:43 Year 3 M4 A4
1944	Jan 6 17:57 Year 3 M3 A5	Feb 5 07:24 Year 2 M2 A5	Mar 6 03:32 Year 2 M1 A6	Apr 4 10:33 Year 2 M9 A7	May 5 06:25 Year 2 M8 A8	June 5 12:43 Year 2 M7 A9	July 7 00:38 Year 2 M6 A1	Aug 7 13:10 Year 2 M5 A2	Sept 7 17:48 Year 2 M4 A3	Oct 8 10:52 Year 2 M3 A4	Nov 7 16:00 Year 2 M2 A5	Dec 7 10:41 Year 2 M1 A6
1945	Jan 5 23:37 Year 2 M9 A7	Feb 4 13:23 Year 1 M8 A7	Mar 6 09:28 Year 1 M7 A8	Apr 4 16:24 Year 1 M6 A9	May 5 12:08 Year 1 M5 A1	June 5 18:21 Year 1 M4 A2	July 7 07:25 Year 1 M3 A3	Aug 7 18:41 Year 1 M2 A4	Sept 7 23:19 Year 1 M1 A5	Oct 8 16:52 Year 1 M9 A6	Nov 7 21:40 Year 1 M8 A7	Dec 7 16:25 Year 1 M7 A8

Year	Jan	Feb	Mar	Apr	May	June	July	Aug	Sept	Oct	Nov	Dec
1946	Jan 6	Feb 4	Mar 6	Apr 4	May 5	June 5	July 7	Aug 8	Sept 8	Oct 8	Nov 8	Dec 7
	05:24	19:11	15:13	22:04	17:40	23:47	12:52	00:11	04:56	22:38	03:32	22:06
	Year 1	Year 9	Year 9	Year 9	Year 9	Year 9	Year 9	Year 9	Year 9	Year 9	Year 9	Year 9
	M6 A9	M5 A9	M4 A1	M3 A2	M2 A3	M1 A4	M9 A5	M8 A6	M7 A7	M6 A8	M5 A9	M4 A1
1947	Jan 6	Feb 5	Mar 6	Apr 5	May 5	June 6	July 7	Aug 8	Sept 8	Oct 9	Nov 8	Dec 8
	11:19	00:48	20:55	04:08	23:09	06:23	18:18	05:43	11:27	04:28	09:29	04:06
	Year 9	Year 8	Year 8	Year 8	Year 8	Year 8	Year 8	Year 8	Year 8	Year 8	Year 8	Year 8
	M3 A2	M2 A2	M1 A3	M9 A4	M8 A5	M7 A6	M6 A7	M5 A8	M4 A9	M3 A1	M2 A2	M1 A3
1948	Jan 6	Feb 5	Mar 6	Apr 4	May 5	June 5	July 6	Aug 7	Sept 7	Oct 8	Nov 7	Dec 7
	17:18	06:43	02:50	09:50	05:39	11:55	23:49	12:21	16:59	10:05	15:13	09:51
	Year 8	Year 7	Year 7	Year 7	Year 7	Year 7	Year 7	Year 7	Year 7	Year 7	Year 7	Year 7
	M9 A4	M8 A4	M7 A5	M6 A6	M5 A7	M4 A8	M3 A9	M2 A1	M1 A2	M9 A3	M8 A4	M7 A5
1949	Jan 5	Feb 4	Mar 6	Apr 4	May 5	June 5	July 7	Aug 7	Sept 7	Oct 8	Nov 7	Dec 7
	22:43	12:26	08:30	15:25	11:11	17:25	05:18	17:52	22:36	16:15	21:05	15:50
	Year 7	Year 6	Year 6	Year 6	Year 6	Year 6	Year 6	Year 6	Year 6	Year 6	Year 6	Year 6
	M6 A6	M5 A6	M4 A7	M3 A8	M2 A9	M1 A1	M9 A2	M8 A3	M7 A4	M6 A5	M5 A6	M4 A7
1950	Jan 6	Feb 4	Mar 6	Apr 4	May 5	June 5	July 7	Aug 7	Sept 8	Oct 8	Nov 8	Dec 7
	04:46	18:27	14:24	21:10	16:46	22:52	11:57	23:17	4:04	21:49	2:49	21:28
	Year 6	Year 5	Year 5	Year 5	Year 5	Year 5	Year 5	Year 5	Year 5	Year 5	Year 5	Year 5
	M3 A8	M2 A8	M1 A9	M9 A1	M8 A2	M7 A3	M6 A4	M5 A5	M4 A6	M3 A7	M2 A8	M1 A9
1951	Jan 6	Feb 5	Mar 6	Apr 5	May 5	June 6	July 7	Aug 8	Sept 8	Oct 9	Nov 8	Dec 8
	10:43	00:11	20:15	03:21	22:18	05:27	17:20	04:43	09:36	03:28	08:31	03:11
	Year 5	Year 4	Year 4	Year 4	Year 4	Year 4	Year 4	Year 4	Year 4	Year 4	Year 4	Year 4
	M9 A1	M8 A1	M7 A2	M6 A3	M5 A4	M4 A5	M3 A6	M2 A7	M1 A8	M9 A9	M8 A1	M7 A2
1952	Jan 6	Feb 5	Mar 6	Apr 4	May 5	June 5	July 6	Aug 7	Sept 7	Oct 8	Nov 7	Dec 7
	16:26	05:53	01:59	08:56	04:43	10:58	22:52	11:28	16:09	09:17	14:25	09:08
	Year 4	Year 3	Year 3	Year 3	Year 3	Year 3	Year 3	Year 3	Year 3	Year 3	Year 3	Year 3
	M6 A3	M5 A3	M4 A4	M3 A5	M2 A6	M1 A7	M9 A8	M8 A9	M7 A1	M6 A2	M5 A3	M4 A4
1953	Jan 5	Feb 4	Mar 6	Apr 4	May 5	June 5	July 7	Aug 7	Sept 7	Oct 8	Nov 7	Dec 7
	22:04	11:49	07:53	14:46	10:28	16:36	04:25	16:55	21:37	15:15	20:07	14:53
	Year 3	Year 2	Year 2	Year 2	Year 2	Year 2	Year 2	Year 2	Year 2	Year 2	Year 2	Year 2
	M3 A5	M2 A5	M1 A6	M9 A7	M8 A8	M7 A9	M6 A1	M5 A2	M4 A3	M3 A4	M2 A5	M1 A6
1954	Jan 6	Feb 4	Mar 6	Apr 4	May 5	June 5	July 7	Aug 7	Sept 8	Oct 8	Nov 8	Dec 7
	03:52	17:37	13:38	20:27	16:01	22:05	11:06	22:24	03:10	20:56	01:55	20:33
	Year 2	Year 1	Year 1	Year 1	Year 1	Year 1	Year 1	Year 1	Year 1	Year 1	Year 1	Year 1
	M9 A7	M8 A7	M7 A8	M6 A9	M5 A1	M4 A2	M3 A3	M2 A4	M1 A5	M9 A6	M8 A7	M7 A8
1955	Jan 6	Feb 4	Mar 6	Apr 5	May 5	June 6	July 7	Aug 8	Sept 8	Oct 9	Nov 8	Dec 8
	09:47	23:14	19:18	02:29	21:28	03:30	16:34	03:58	08:51	02:44	07:50	02:31
	Year 1	Year 9	Year 9	Year 9	Year 9	Year 9	Year 9	Year 9	Year 9	Year 9	Year 9	Year 9
	M6 A9	M5 A9	M4 A1	M3 A2	M2 A3	M1 A4	M9 A5	M8 A6	M7 A7	M6 A8	M5 A9	M4 A1
1956	Jan 6	Feb 5	Mar 6	Apr 4	May 5	June 5	July 6	Aug 7	Sept 7	Oct 8	Nov 7	Dec 7
	15:46	05:11	01:17	00:14	04:00	10:16	22:08	10:39	12:15	08:22	13:30	08:14
	Year 9	Year 8	Year 8	Year 8	Year 8	Year 8	Year 8	Year 8	Year 8	Year 8	Year 8	Year 8
	M3 A2	M2 A2	M1 A3	M9 A4	M8 A5	M7 A6	M6 A7	M5 A8	M4 A9	M3 A1	M2 A2	M1 A3
1957	Jan 5	Feb 4	Mar 6	Apr 4	May 5	June 5	July 7	Aug 7	Sept 7	Oct 8	Nov 7	Dec 7
	21:12	10:57	07:01	13:54	09:36	15:47	03:40	16:14	20:57	14:35	19:26	14:11
	Year 8	Year 7	Year 7	Year 7	Year 7	Year 7	Year 7	Year 7	Year 7	Year 7	Year 7	Year 7
	M9 A4	M8 A4	M7 A5	M6 A6	M5 A7	M4 A8	M3 A9	M2 A1	M1 A2	M9 A3	M8 A4	M7 A5
1958	Jan 6	Feb 4	Mar 6	Apr 4	May 5	June 5	July 7	Aug 7	Sept 8	Oct 8	Nov 8	Dec 7
	03:10	16:54	09:43	19:40	15:14	21:18	10:22	21:43	02:32	20:19	01:17	19:54
	Year 7	Year 6	Year 6	Year 6	Year 6	Year 6	Year 6	Year 6	Year 6	Year 6	Year 6	Year 6
	M6 A6	M5 A6	M4 A7	M3 A8	M2 A9	M1 A1	M9 A2	M8 A3	M7 A4	M6 A5	M5 A6	M4 A7
1959	Jan 6	Feb 4	Mar 6	Apr 5	May 5	June 6	July 7	Aug 8	Sept 8	Oct 9	Nov 8	Dec 8
	09:09	22:38	18:45	01:54	20:51	02:50	15:51	03:14	08:09	02:03	07:07	01:45
	Year 6	Year 5	Year 5	Year 5	Year 5	Year 5	Year 5	Year 5	Year 5	Year 5	Year 5	Year 5
	M3 A8	M2 A8	M1 A9	M9 A1	M8 A2	M7 A3	M6 A4	M5 A5	M4 A6	M3 A7	M2 A8	M1 A9
1960	Jan 6	Feb 5	Mar 6	Apr 4	May 5	June 5	July 6	Aug 7	Sept 7	Oct 8	Nov 7	Dec 7
	14:58	04:23	00:29	07:27	03:15	09:30	21:25	10:01	14:44	07:55	13:05	07:49
	Year 5	Year 4	Year 4	Year 4	Year 4	Year 4	Year 4	Year 4	Year 4	Year 4	Year 4	Year 4
	M9 A1	M8 A1	M7 A2	M6 A3	M5 A4	M4 A5	M3 A6	M2 A7	M1 A8	M9 A9	M8 A1	M7 A2
1961	Jan 5	Feb 4	Mar 6	Apr 4	May 5	June 5	July 7	Aug 7	Sept 7	Oct 8	Nov 7	Dec 7
	20:43	10:25	6:25	13:18	9:00	15:11	3:01	15:33	20:16	13:57	18:52	13:41
	Year 4	Year 3	Year 3	Year 3	Year 3	Year 3	Year 3	Year 3	Year 3	Year 3	Year 3	Year 3
	M6 A3	M5 A3	M4 A4	M3 A5	M2 A6	M1 A7	M9 A8	M8 A9	M7 A1	M6 A2	M5 A3	M4 A4
1962	Jan 6	Feb 4	Mar 6	Apr 4	May 5	June 5	July 7	Aug 7	Sept 8	Oct 8	Nov 8	Dec 7
	02:41	16:23	12:19	19:03	14:36	20:40	9:42	21:02	01:50	19:38	00:40	19:21
	Year 3	Year 2	Year 2	Year 2	Year 2	Year 2	Year 2	Year 2	Year 2	Year 2	Year 2	Year 2
	M3 A5	M2 A5	M1 A6	M9 A7	M8 A8	M7 A9	M6 A1	M5 A2	M4 A3	M3 A4	M2 A5	M1 A6
1963	Jan 6	Feb 4	Mar 6	Apr 5	May 5	June 6	July 7	Aug 8	Sept 8	Oct 9	Nov 8	Dec 8
	08:37	22:04	18:05	01:10	20:05	02:06	15:10	02:37	07:34	01:30	06:37	01:21
	Year 2	Year 1	Year 1	Year 1	Year 1	Year 1	Year 1	Year 1	Year 1	Year 1	Year 1	Year 1
	M9 A7	M8 A7	M7 A8	M6 A9	M5 A1	M4 A2	M3 A3	M2 A4	M1 A5	M9 A6	M8 A7	M7 A8

Year	Jan	Feb	Mar	Apr	May	June	July	Aug	Sept	Oct	Nov	Dec
1964	Jan 6	Feb 5	Mar 6	Apr 4	May 5	June 5	July 6	Aug 7	Sept 7	Oct 8	Nov 7	Dec 7
	14:38	04:04	00:08	07:02	01:51	08:55	20:47	09:19	15:25	07:09	12:19	07:05
	Year 1	Year 9	Year 9	Year 9	Year 9	Year 9	Year 9	Year 9	Year 9	Year 9	Year 9	Year 9
	M6 A9	M5 A9	M4 A1	M3 A2	M2 A3	M1 A4	M9 A5	M8 A6	M7 A7	M6 A8	M5 A9	M4 A1
1965	Jan 5	Feb 4	Mar 6	Apr 4	May 5	June 5	July 7	Aug 7	Sept 7	Oct 8	Nov 7	Dec 7
	20:02	09:48	05:52	12:44	08:22	14:29	02:18	14:51	19:36	13:18	18:12	13:00
	Year 9	Year 8	Year 8	Year 8	Year 8	Year 8	Year 8	Year 8	Year 8	Year 8	Year 8	Year 8
	M3 A2	M2 A2	M1 A3	M9 A4	M8 A5	M7 A6	M6 A7	M5 A8	M4 A9	M3 A1	M2 A2	M1 A3
1966	Jan 6	Feb 4	Mar 6	Apr 4	May 5	June 5	July 7	Aug 7	Sept 8	Oct 8	Nov 8	Dec 7
	01:59	15:42	11:41	18:26	13:58	20:00	09:00	20:19	01:08	18:58	00:00	18:42
	Year 8	Year 7	Year 7	Year 7	Year 7	Year 7	Year 7	Year 7	Year 7	Year 7	Year 7	Year 7
	M9 A4	M8 A4	M7 A5	M6 A6	M5 A7	M4 A8	M3 A9	M2 A1	M1 A2	M9 A3	M8 A4	M7 A5
1967	Jan 6	Feb 4	Mar 6	Apr 5	May 5	June 6	July 7	Aug 8	Sept 8	Oct 9	Nov 8	Dec 8
	07:58	21:26	17:30	00:07	19:33	01:30	14:29	01:49	06:42	00:36	05:42	00:25
	Year 7	Year 6	Year 6	Year 6	Year 6	Year 6	Year 6	Year 6	Year 6	Year 6	Year 6	Year 6
	M6 A6	M5 A6	M4 A7	M3 A8	M2 A9	M1 A1	M9 A2	M8 A3	M7 A4	M6 A5	M5 A6	M4 A7
1968	Jan 6	Feb 5	Mar 5	Apr 4	May 5	June 5	July 6	Aug 7	Sept 7	Oct 8	Nov 7	Dec 7
	13:41	03:06	23:11	06:06	0:58	08:05	19:59	07:24	13:13	06:22	11:33	06:19
	Year 6	Year 5	Year 5	Year 5	Year 5	Year 5	Year 5	Year 5	Year 5	Year 5	Year 5	Year 5
	M3 A8	M2 A8	M1 A9	M9 A1	M8 A2	M7 A3	M6 A4	M5 A5	M4 A6	M3 A7	M2 A8	M1 A9
1969	Jan 5	Feb 4	Mar 6	Apr 4	May 5	June 5	July 7	Aug 7	Sept 7	Oct 8	Nov 7	Dec 7
	19:16	09:00	05:02	11:53	07:32	13:41	01:30	14:03	18:45	11:59	17:17	12:06
	Year 5	Year 4	Year 4	Year 4	Year 4	Year 4	Year 4	Year 4	Year 4	Year 4	Year 4	Year 4
	M9 A1	M8 A1	M7 A2	M6 A3	M5 A4	M4 A5	M3 A6	M2 A7	M1 A8	M9 A9	M8 A1	M7 A2
1970	Jan 6	Feb 4	Mar 6	Apr 4	May 5	June 5	July 7	Aug 7	Sept 8	Oct 8	Nov 7	Dec 7
	01:21	14:51	10:48	17:33	13:04	19:06	08:07	19:27	00:16	18:03	23:03	17:41
	Year 4	Year 3	Year 3	Year 3	Year 3	Year 3	Year 3	Year 3	Year 3	Year 3	Year 3	Year 3
	M6 A3	M5 A3	M4 A4	M3 A5	M2 A6	M1 A7	M9 A8	M8 A9	M7 A1	M6 A2	M5 A3	M4 A4
1971	Jan 6	Feb 4	Mar 6	Apr 4	May 5	June 6	July 7	Aug 8	Sept 8	Oct 8	Nov 8	Dec 7
	06:54	06:02	16:23	23:00	18:25	00:26	13:30	00:56	05:56	23:54	05:01	23:43
	Year 3	Year 2	Year 2	Year 2	Year 2	Year 2	Year 2	Year 2	Year 2	Year 2	Year 2	Year 2
	M3 A5	M2 A5	M1 A6	M9 A7	M8 A8	M7 A9	M6 A1	M5 A2	M4 A3	M3 A4	M2 A5	M1 A6
1972	Jan 6	Feb 5	Mar 5	Apr 4	May 5	June 5	July 6	Aug 7	Sept 7	Oct 8	Nov 7	Dec 7
	12:56	02:18	22:15	05:15	00:05	07:11	19:03	06:29	12:19	05:31	10:44	05:29
	Year 2	Year 1	Year 1	Year 1	Year 1	Year 1	Year 1	Year 1	Year 1	Year 1	Year 1	Year 1
	M9 A7	M8 A7	M7 A8	M6 A9	M5 A1	M4 A2	M3 A3	M2 A4	M1 A5	M9 A6	M8 A7	M7 A8
1973	Jan 5	Feb 4	Mar 6	Apr 4	May 5	June 5	July 7	Aug 7	Sept 7	Oct 8	Nov 7	Dec 7
	18:45	08:06	04:04	10:53	06:31	12:39	00:30	13:05	17:51	11:09	16:33	11:24
	Year 1	Year 9	Year 9	Year 9	Year 9	Year 9	Year 9	Year 9	Year 9	Year 9	Year 9	Year 9
	M6 A9	M5 A9	M4 A1	M3 A2	M2 A3	M1 A4	M9 A5	M8 A6	M7 A7	M6 A8	M5 A9	M4 A1
1974	Jan 6	Feb 4	Mar 6	Apr 4	May 5	June 5	July 7	Aug 7	Sept 7	Oct 8	Nov 7	Dec 7
	00:23	14:04	09:57	16:37	12:06	18:07	07:11	18:32	23:25	17:17	22:23	17:08
	Year 9	Year 8	Year 8	Year 8	Year 8	Year 8	Year 8	Year 8	Year 8	Year 8	Year 8	Year 8
	M3 A2	M2 A2	M1 A3	M9 A4	M8 A5	M7 A6	M6 A7	M5 A8	M4 A9	M3 A1	M2 A2	M1 A3
1975	Jan 6	Feb 4	Mar 6	Apr 4	May 5	June 5	July 7	Aug 8	Sept 8	Oct 8	Nov 8	Dec 7
	06:26	20:07	15:55	22:26	17:22	23:41	12:41	00:05	05:01	22:59	04:07	22:53
	Year 8	Year 7	Year 7	Year 7	Year 7	Year 7	Year 7	Year 7	Year 7	Year 7	Year 7	Year 7
	M9 A4	M8 A4	M7 A5	M6 A6	M5 A7	M4 A8	M3 A9	M2 A1	M1 A2	M9 A3	M8 A4	M7 A5
1976	Jan 6	Feb 5	Mar 5	Apr 4	May 4	June 5	July 6	Aug 7	Sept 7	Oct 8	Nov 7	Dec 7
	12:11	01:37	21:36	04:34	23:21	06:23	18:14	05:41	11:33	04:48	10:02	04:51
	Year 7	Year 6	Year 6	Year 6	Year 6	Year 6	Year 6	Year 6	Year 6	Year 6	Year 6	Year 6
	M6 A6	M5 A6	M4 A7	M3 A8	M2 A9	M1 A1	M9 A2	M8 A3	M7 A4	M6 A5	M5 A6	M4 A7
1977	Jan 5	Feb 4	Mar 6	Apr 4	May 5	June 5	July 6	Aug 7	Sept 7	Oct 8	Nov 7	Dec 7
	18:09	07:34	03:36	10:25	06:02	12:06	23:52	12:24	17:09	10:19	15:52	10:44
	Year 6	Year 5	Year 5	Year 5	Year 5	Year 5	Year 5	Year 5	Year 5	Year 5	Year 5	Year 5
	M3 A8	M2 A8	M1 A9	M9 A1	M8 A2	M7 A3	M6 A4	M5 A5	M4 A6	M3 A7	M2 A8	M1 A9
1978	Jan 5	Feb 4	Mar 6	Apr 4	May 5	June 5	July 7	Aug 7	Sept 7	Oct 8	Nov 7	Dec 7
	23:46	13:31	09:28	16:12	11:42	17:41	05:24	17:55	22:44	16:34	21:39	16:37
	Year 5	Year 4	Year 4	Year 4	Year 4	Year 4	Year 4	Year 4	Year 4	Year 4	Year 4	Year 4
	M9 A1	M8 A1	M7 A2	M6 A3	M5 A4	M4 A5	M3 A6	M2 A7	M1 A8	M9 A9	M8 A1	M7 A2
1979	Jan 6	Feb 4	Mar 6	Apr 4	May 5	June 5	July 7	Aug 7	Sept 8	Oct 8	Nov 8	Dec 7
	05:39	19:19	15:09	21:44	17:07	23:06	12:08	23:32	04:28	22:27	03:37	22:24
	Year 4	Year 3	Year 3	Year 3	Year 3	Year 3	Year 3	Year 3	Year 3	Year 3	Year 3	Year 3
	M6 A3	M5 A3	M4 A4	M3 A5	M2 A6	M1 A7	M9 A8	M8 A9	M7 A1	M6 A2	M5 A3	M4 A4
1980	Jan 6	Feb 5	Mar 5	Apr 4	May 4	June 5	July 6	Aug 7	Sept 7	Oct 8	Nov 7	Dec 7
	11:41	01:07	21:04	04:02	22:52	05:57	17:48	05:13	10:11	04:10	09:23	04:11
	Year 3	Year 2	Year 2	Year 2	Year 2	Year 2	Year 2	Year 2	Year 2	Year 2	Year 2	Year 2
	M3 A5	M2 A5	M1 A6	M9 A7	M8 A8	M7 A9	M6 A1	M5 A2	M4 A3	M3 A4	M2 A5	M1 A6
1981	Jan 5	Feb 4	Mar 6	Apr 4	May 5	June 5	July 6	Aug 7	Sept 7	Oct 8	Nov 7	Dec 7
	17:31	06:56	02:57	09:46	05:22	11:29	23:18	11:53	16:38	09:53	15:14	10:04
	Year 2	Year 1	Year 1	Year 1	Year 1	Year 1	Year 1	Year 1	Year 1	Year 1	Year 1	Year 1
	M9 A7	M8 A7	M7 A8	M6 A9	M5 A1	M4 A2	M3 A3	M2 A4	M1 A5	M9 A6	M8 A7	M7 A8

Year	Jan	Feb	Mar	Apr	May	June	July	Aug	Sept	Oct	Nov	Dec
1982	Jan 5 / 23:05 / Year 1 / M6 A9	Feb 4 / 12:49 / Year 9 / M5 A9	Mar 6 / 08:45 / Year 9 / M4 A1	Apr 4 / 15:26 / Year 9 / M3 A2	May 5 / 10:54 / Year 9 / M2 A3	June 5 / 16:55 / Year 9 / M1 A4	July 7 / 04:42 / Year 9 / M9 A5	Aug 7 / 17:21 / Year 9 / M8 A6	Sept 7 / 22:14 / Year 9 / M7 A7	Oct 8 / 16:06 / Year 9 / M6 A8	Nov 7 / 21:10 / Year 9 / M5 A9	Dec 7 / 16:04 / Year 9 / M4 A1
1983	Jan 6 / 05:06 / Year 9 / M3 A2	Feb 4 / 18:46 / Year 8 / M2 A2	Mar 6 / 14:36 / Year 8 / M1 A3	Apr 6 / 21:11 / Year 8 / M9 A4	May 6 / 16:33 / Year 8 / M8 A5	June 6 / 22:28 / Year 8 / M7 A6	July 7 / 11:28 / Year 8 / M6 A7	Aug 7 / 22:53 / Year 8 / M5 A8	Sept 8 / 03:51 / Year 8 / M4 A9	Oct 8 / 21:49 / Year 8 / M3 A1	Nov 8 / 02:57 / Year 8 / M2 A2	Dec 7 / 21:40 / Year 8 / M1 A3
1984	Jan 6 / 10:54 / Year 8 / M9 A4	Feb 5 / 00:16 / Year 7 / M8 A4	Mar 5 / 20:13 / Year 7 / M7 A5	Apr 4 / 03:11 / Year 7 / M6 A6	May 5 / 22:01 / Year 7 / M5 A7	June 5 / 05:04 / Year 7 / M4 A8	July 6 / 16:56 / Year 7 / M3 A9	Aug 7 / 04:24 / Year 7 / M2 A1	Sept 7 / 09:27 / Year 7 / M1 A2	Oct 8 / 03:33 / Year 7 / M9 A3	Nov 7 / 08:49 / Year 7 / M8 A4	Dec 7 / 03:37 / Year 7 / M7 A5
1985	Jan 5 / 16:52 / Year 7 / M6 A6	Feb 4 / 06:12 / Year 6 / M5 A6	Mar 6 / 02:08 / Year 6 / M4 A7	Apr 5 / 08:55 / Year 6 / M3 A8	May 5 / 04:32 / Year 6 / M2 A9	June 5 / 10:38 / Year 6 / M1 A1	July 6 / 22:27 / Year 6 / M9 A2	Aug 7 / 11:02 / Year 6 / M8 A3	Sept 7 / 15:49 / Year 6 / M7 A4	Oct 8 / 09:09 / Year 6 / M6 A5	Nov 7 / 14:33 / Year 6 / M5 A6	Dec 7 / 09:29 / Year 6 / M4 A7
1986	Jan 5 / 22:30 / Year 6 / M3 A8	Feb 4 / 12:11 / Year 5 / M2 A8	Mar 6 / 08:03 / Year 5 / M1 A9	Apr 4 / 14:41 / Year 5 / M9 A1	May 5 / 10:07 / Year 5 / M8 A2	June 5 / 16:07 / Year 5 / M7 A3	July 7 / 03:52 / Year 5 / M6 A4	Aug 7 / 16:28 / Year 5 / M5 A5	Sept 7 / 21:19 / Year 5 / M4 A6	Oct 8 / 15:12 / Year 5 / M3 A7	Nov 7 / 20:18 / Year 5 / M2 A8	Dec 7 / 15:18 / Year 5 / M1 A9
1987	Jan 6 / 04:20 / Year 5 / M9 A1	Feb 4 / 17:58 / Year 4 / M8 A1	Mar 6 / 13:43 / Year 4 / M7 A2	Apr 4 / 20:12 / Year 4 / M6 A3	May 5 / 15:30 / Year 4 / M5 A4	June 5 / 21:25 / Year 4 / M4 A5	July 7 / 10:27 / Year 4 / M3 A6	Aug 7 / 21:54 / Year 4 / M2 A7	Sept 7 / 02:56 / Year 4 / M1 A8	Oct 8 / 20:58 / Year 4 / M9 A9	Nov 7 / 02:10 / Year 4 / M8 A1	Dec 7 / 20:57 / Year 4 / M7 A2
1988	Jan 6 / 10:15 / Year 4 / M6 A3	Feb 4 / 23:40 / Year 3 / M5 A3	Mar 5 / 19:34 / Year 3 / M4 A4	Apr 4 / 02:29 / Year 3 / M3 A5	May 4 / 21:12 / Year 3 / M2 A6	June 5 / 03:03 / Year 3 / M1 A7	July 6 / 16:03 / Year 3 / M9 A8	Aug 7 / 03:29 / Year 3 / M8 A9	Sept 7 / 08:32 / Year 3 / M7 A1	Oct 8 / 02:37 / Year 3 / M6 A2	Nov 7 / 07:53 / Year 3 / M5 A3	Dec 7 / 02:43 / Year 3 / M4 A4
1989	Jan 5 / 16:03 / Year 3 / M3 A5	Feb 4 / 05:27 / Year 2 / M2 A5	Mar 6 / 01:26 / Year 2 / M1 A6	Apr 4 / 08:13 / Year 2 / M9 A7	May 5 / 03:45 / Year 2 / M8 A8	June 5 / 09:47 / Year 2 / M7 A9	July 6 / 21:32 / Year 2 / M6 A1	Aug 7 / 10:04 / Year 2 / M5 A2	Sept 7 / 14:52 / Year 2 / M4 A3	Oct 8 / 08:13 / Year 2 / M3 A4	Nov 7 / 13:37 / Year 2 / M2 A5	Dec 7 / 08:33 / Year 2 / M1 A6
1990	Jan 5 / 21:34 / Year 2 / M9 A7	Feb 4 / 11:17 / Year 1 / M8 A7	Mar 6 / 07:10 / Year 1 / M7 A8	Apr 5 / 13:48 / Year 1 / M6 A9	May 5 / 09:14 / Year 1 / M5 A1	June 5 / 15:11 / Year 1 / M4 A2	July 7 / 02:55 / Year 1 / M3 A3	Aug 7 / 15:30 / Year 1 / M2 A4	Sept 7 / 20:24 / Year 1 / M1 A5	Oct 8 / 14:20 / Year 1 / M9 A6	Nov 7 / 19:29 / Year 1 / M8 A7	Dec 7 / 14:29 / Year 1 / M7 A8
1991	Jan 6 / 03:34 / Year 1 / M6 A9	Feb 4 / 17:14 / Year 9 / M5 A9	Mar 6 / 13:02 / Year 9 / M4 A1	Apr 4 / 19:33 / Year 9 / M3 A2	May 5 / 14:53 / Year 9 / M2 A3	June 5 / 20:46 / Year 9 / M1 A4	July 7 / 09:44 / Year 9 / M9 A5	Aug 7 / 21:06 / Year 9 / M8 A6	Sept 8 / 02:02 / Year 9 / M7 A7	Oct 8 / 20:01 / Year 9 / M6 A8	Nov 8 / 01:13 / Year 9 / M5 A9	Dec 7 / 20:01 / Year 9 / M4 A1
1992	Jan 6 / 09:20 / Year 9 / M3 A2	Feb 4 / 22:45 / Year 8 / M2 A2	Mar 6 / 18:41 / Year 8 / M1 A3	Apr 4 / 01:36 / Year 8 / M9 A4	May 4 / 20:22 / Year 8 / M8 A5	June 5 / 02:14 / Year 8 / M7 A6	July 6 / 15:13 / Year 8 / M6 A7	Aug 7 / 02:39 / Year 8 / M5 A8	Sept 7 / 07:40 / Year 8 / M4 A9	Oct 8 / 01:44 / Year 8 / M3 A1	Nov 7 / 07:01 / Year 8 / M2 A2	Dec 7 / 01:52 / Year 8 / M1 A3
1993	Jan 5 / 15:12 / Year 8 / M9 A4	Feb 4 / 04:37 / Year 7 / M8 A4	Mar 6 / 00:35 / Year 7 / M7 A5	Apr 4 / 07:21 / Year 7 / M6 A6	May 5 / 02:55 / Year 7 / M5 A7	June 5 / 08:59 / Year 7 / M4 A8	July 6 / 20:46 / Year 7 / M3 A9	Aug 7 / 09:21 / Year 7 / M2 A1	Sept 7 / 14:08 / Year 7 / M1 A2	Oct 8 / 07:27 / Year 7 / M9 A3	Nov 7 / 12:49 / Year 7 / M8 A4	Dec 7 / 07:45 / Year 7 / M7 A5
1994	Jan 5 / 20:49 / Year 7 / M6 A6	Feb 4 / 10:33 / Year 6 / M5 A6	Mar 6 / 06:29 / Year 6 / M4 A7	Apr 4 / 13:08 / Year 6 / M3 A8	May 5 / 08:34 / Year 6 / M2 A9	June 5 / 14:32 / Year 6 / M1 A1	July 7 / 02:16 / Year 6 / M9 A2	Aug 7 / 14:51 / Year 6 / M8 A3	Sept 7 / 19:43 / Year 6 / M7 A4	Oct 8 / 13:36 / Year 6 / M6 A5	Nov 7 / 18:41 / Year 6 / M5 A6	Dec 7 / 13:38 / Year 6 / M4 A7
1995	Jan 6 / 02:39 / Year 6 / M3 A8	Feb 4 / 16:19 / Year 5 / M2 A8	Mar 6 / 12:06 / Year 5 / M1 A9	Apr 4 / 18:38 / Year 5 / M9 A1	May 5 / 13:58 / Year 5 / M8 A2	June 5 / 19:53 / Year 5 / M7 A3	July 7 / 08:54 / Year 5 / M6 A4	Aug 7 / 20:22 / Year 5 / M5 A5	Sept 8 / 01:24 / Year 5 / M4 A6	Oct 8 / 19:27 / Year 5 / M3 A7	Nov 8 / 00:40 / Year 5 / M2 A8	Dec 7 / 19:27 / Year 5 / M1 A9
1996	Jan 6 / 08:42 / Year 5 / M9 A1	Feb 4 / 22:04 / Year 4 / M8 A1	Mar 5 / 17:58 / Year 4 / M7 A2	Apr 4 / 00:54 / Year 4 / M6 A3	May 4 / 19:40 / Year 4 / M5 A4	June 5 / 01:34 / Year 4 / M4 A5	July 6 / 14:35 / Year 4 / M3 A6	Aug 7 / 02:02 / Year 4 / M2 A7	Sept 7 / 07:06 / Year 4 / M1 A8	Oct 8 / 01:12 / Year 4 / M9 A9	Nov 7 / 06:31 / Year 4 / M8 A1	Dec 7 / 01:22 / Year 4 / M7 A2
1997	Jan 5 / 14:40 / Year 4 / M6 A3	Feb 4 / 04:01 / Year 3 / M5 A3	Mar 5 / 23:57 / Year 3 / M4 A4	Apr 4 / 06:41 / Year 3 / M3 A5	May 5 / 01:22 / Year 3 / M2 A6	June 5 / 08:18 / Year 3 / M1 A7	July 6 / 20:07 / Year 3 / M9 A8	Aug 7 / 07:34 / Year 3 / M8 A9	Sept 7 / 13:30 / Year 3 / M7 A1	Oct 8 / 06:52 / Year 3 / M6 A2	Nov 7 / 12:18 / Year 3 / M5 A3	Dec 7 / 07:16 / Year 3 / M4 A4
1998	Jan 5 / 20:18 / Year 3 / M3 A5	Feb 4 / 09:59 / Year 2 / M2 A5	Mar 6 / 05:48 / Year 2 / M1 A6	Apr 4 / 12:22 / Year 2 / M9 A7	May 5 / 07:45 / Year 2 / M8 A8	June 5 / 13:43 / Year 2 / M7 A9	July 7 / 01:29 / Year 2 / M6 A1	Aug 7 / 14:08 / Year 2 / M5 A2	Sept 7 / 19:05 / Year 2 / M4 A3	Oct 8 / 12:36 / Year 2 / M3 A4	Nov 7 / 18:14 / Year 2 / M2 A5	Dec 7 / 13:16 / Year 2 / M1 A6
1999	Jan 6 / 02:22 / Year 2 / M9 A7	Feb 4 / 16:02 / Year 1 / M8 A7	Mar 6 / 11:47 / Year 1 / M7 A8	Apr 4 / 18:14 / Year 1 / M6 A9	May 5 / 13:30 / Year 1 / M5 A1	June 5 / 19:21 / Year 1 / M4 A2	July 7 / 08:21 / Year 1 / M3 A3	Aug 7 / 19:46 / Year 1 / M2 A4	Sept 8 / 00:47 / Year 1 / M1 A5	Oct 8 / 18:49 / Year 1 / M9 A6	Nov 8 / 00:03 / Year 1 / M8 A7	Dec 7 / 18:52 / Year 1 / M7 A8

Year	Jan	Feb	Mar	Apr	May	June	July	Aug	Sept	Oct	Nov	Dec
2000	Jan 6	Feb 4	Mar 5	Apr 3	May 4	June 5	July 6	Aug 7	Sept 7	Oct 8	Nov 7	Dec 7
	08:12	21:36	17:32	23:57	19:08	00:56	13:51	01:19	06:23	00:33	05:52	00:45
	Year 1	Year 9	Year 9	Year 9	Year 9	Year 9	Year 9	Year 9	Year 9	Year 9	Year 9	Year 9
	M6 A9	M5 A9	M4 A1	M3 A2	M2 A3	M1 A4	M9 A5	M8 A6	M7 A7	M6 A8	M5 A9	M4 A1
2001	Jan 5	Feb 4	Mar 5	Apr 4	May 5	June 5	July 6	Aug 7	Sept 7	Oct 8	Nov 7	Dec 7
	14:05	03:29	23:26	06:10	00:48	07:42	19:26	06:52	12:50	06:14	11:41	06:41
	Year 9	Year 8	Year 8	Year 8	Year 8	Year 8	Year 8	Year 8	Year 8	Year 8	Year 8	Year 8
	M3 A2	M2 A2	M1 A3	M9 A4	M8 A5	M7 A6	M6 A7	M5 A8	M4 A9	M3 A1	M2 A2	M1 A3
2002	Jan 5	Feb 4	Mar 6	Apr 4	May 5	June 5	July 7	Aug 7	Sept 7	Oct 8	Nov 7	Dec 7
	19:45	09:27	05:20	11:57	07:21	13:17	00:59	13:31	18:23	11:52	17:29	12:30
	Year 8	Year 7	Year 7	Year 7	Year 7	Year 7	Year 7	Year 7	Year 7	Year 7	Year 7	Year 7
	M9 A4	M8 A4	M7 A5	M6 A6	M5 A7	M4 A8	M3 A9	M2 A1	M1 A2	M9 A3	M8 A4	M7 A5
2003	Jan 6	Feb 4	Mar 6	Apr 4	May 5	June 5	July 7	Aug 7	Sept 8	Oct 8	Nov 7	Dec 7
	01:34	15:12	10:56	17:25	12:42	18:35	07:35	18:59	00:00	18:03	23:19	18:10
	Year 7	Year 6	Year 6	Year 6	Year 6	Year 6	Year 6	Year 6	Year 6	Year 6	Year 6	Year 6
	M6 A6	M5 A6	M4 A7	M3 A8	M2 A9	M1 A1	M9 A2	M8 A3	M7 A4	M6 A5	M5 A6	M4 A7
2004	Jan 6	Feb 3	Mar 5	Apr 3	May 4	June 5	July 6	Aug 7	Sept 7	Oct 7	Nov 7	Dec 6
	07:29	21:09	16:45	23:08	18:21	00:12	13:12	00:38	05:40	23:46	05:04	23:57
	Year 6	Year 5	Year 5	Year 5	Year 5	Year 5	Year 5	Year 5	Year 5	Year 5	Year 5	Year 5
	M3 A8	M2 A8	M1 A9	M9 A1	M8 A2	M7 A3	M6 A4	M5 A5	M4 A6	M3 A7	M2 A8	M1 A9
2005	Jan 5	Feb 4	Mar 5	Apr 4	May 4	June 5	July 6	Aug 7	Sept 7	Oct 8	Nov 7	Dec 7
	13:18	02:43	22:34	05:22	23:59	06:53	18:39	06:06	12:02	05:23	10:47	05:44
	Year 5	Year 4	Year 4	Year 4	Year 4	Year 4	Year 4	Year 4	Year 4	Year 4	Year 4	Year 4
	M9 A1	M8 A1	M7 A2	M6 A3	M5 A4	M4 A5	M3 A6	M2 A7	M1 A8	M9 A9	M8 A1	M7 A2
2006	Jan 5	Feb 4	Mar 6	Apr 4	May 5	June 5	July 6	Aug 7	Sept 7	Oct 8	Nov 7	Dec 7
	18:51	08:30	04:21	10:56	06:17	12:12	23:56	12:35	17:32	11:04	16:42	11:41
	Year 4	Year 3	Year 3	Year 3	Year 3	Year 3	Year 3	Year 3	Year 3	Year 3	Year 3	Year 3
	M6 A3	M5 A3	M4 A4	M3 A5	M2 A6	M1 A7	M9 A8	M8 A9	M7 A1	M6 A2	M5 A3	M4 A4
2007	Jan 6	Feb 4	Mar 6	Apr 4	May 5	June 5	July 7	Aug 7	Sept 7	Oct 8	Nov 7	Dec 7
	00:45	14:23	10:09	16:38	11:54	17:45	05:29	18:09	23:11	17:15	22:30	17:19
	Year 3	Year 2	Year 2	Year 2	Year 2	Year 2	Year 2	Year 2	Year 2	Year 2	Year 2	Year 2
	M3 A5	M2 A5	M1 A6	M9 A7	M8 A8	M7 A9	M6 A1	M5 A2	M4 A3	M3 A4	M2 A5	M1 A6
2008	Jan 6	Feb 4	Mar 5	Apr 3	May 4	June 4	July 6	Aug 6	Sept 7	Oct 7	Nov 7	Dec 6
	06:35	20:10	15:49	22:13	17:25	23:14	12:11	23:38	04:43	22:54	04:16	23:10
	Year 2	Year 1	Year 1	Year 1	Year 1	Year 1	Year 1	Year 1	Year 1	Year 1	Year 1	Year 1
	M9 A7	M8 A7	M7 A8	M6 A9	M5 A1	M4 A2	M3 A3	M2 A4	M1 A5	M9 A6	M8 A7	M7 A8
2009	Jan 5	Feb 4	Mar 5	Apr 4	May 4	June 5	July 6	Aug 7	Sept 7	Oct 8	Nov 7	Dec 7
	12:29	01:49	21:36	04:22	22:59	05:53	17:39	05:06	10:14	04:30	10:01	05:03
	Year 1	Year 9	Year 9	Year 9	Year 9	Year 9	Year 9	Year 9	Year 9	Year 9	Year 9	Year 9
	M6 A9	M5 A9	M4 A1	M3 A2	M2 A3	M1 A4	M9 A5	M8 A6	M7 A7	M6 A8	M5 A9	M4 A1
2010	Jan 5	Feb 4	Mar 6	Apr 4	May 5	June 5	July 6	Aug 7	Sept 7	Oct 8	Nov 7	Dec 7
	18:28	07:50	03:39	10:12	05:32	11:26	23:10	11:46	16:40	10:11	15:49	10:53
	Year 9	Year 8	Year 8	Year 8	Year 8	Year 8	Year 8	Year 8	Year 8	Year 8	Year 8	Year 8
	M3 A2	M2 A2	M1 A3	M9 A4	M8 A5	M7 A6	M6 A7	M5 A8	M4 A9	M3 A1	M2 A2	M1 A3
2011	Jan 5	Feb 4	Mar 6	Apr 4	May 5	June 5	July 7	Aug 7	Sept 7	Oct 8	Nov 7	Dec 7
	23:59	13:39	09:21	15:47	10:59	16:49	04:32	17:14	22:18	16:24	21:41	16:46
	Year 8	Year 7	Year 7	Year 7	Year 7	Year 7	Year 7	Year 7	Year 7	Year 7	Year 7	Year 7
	M9 A4	M8 A4	M7 A5	M6 A6	M5 A7	M4 A8	M3 A9	M2 A1	M1 A2	M9 A3	M8 A4	M7 A5
2012	Jan 6	Feb 4	Mar 5	Apr 3	May 4	June 4	July 6	Aug 6	Sept 7	Oct 7	Nov 7	Dec 6
	05:53	19:30	15:11	21:33	16:42	22:29	11:27	22:54	03:59	22:10	03:31	22:26
	Year 7	Year 6	Year 6	Year 6	Year 6	Year 6	Year 6	Year 6	Year 6	Year 6	Year 6	Year 6
	M6 A6	M5 A6	M4 A7	M3 A8	M2 A9	M1 A1	M9 A2	M8 A3	M7 A4	M6 A5	M5 A6	M4 A7
2013	Jan 5	Feb 4	Mar 5	Apr 4	May 4	June 5	July 6	Aug 7	Sept 7	Oct 8	Nov 7	Dec 7
	11:48	01:12	21:04	03:52	22:28	05:19	17:03	04:28	09:35	03:50	09:19	04:19
	Year 6	Year 5	Year 5	Year 5	Year 5	Year 5	Year 5	Year 5	Year 5	Year 5	Year 5	Year 5
	M3 A8	M2 A8	M1 A9	M9 A1	M8 A2	M7 A3	M6 A4	M5 A5	M4 A6	M3 A7	M2 A8	M1 A9
2014	Jan 5	Feb 4	Mar 6	Apr 4	May 5	June 5	July 6	Aug 7	Sept 7	Oct 8	Nov 7	Dec 7
	17:43	07:05	02:55	09:29	04:49	10:43	22:25	11:01	15:58	09:32	15:14	10:18
	Year 5	Year 4	Year 4	Year 4	Year 4	Year 4	Year 4	Year 4	Year 4	Year 4	Year 4	Year 4
	M9 A1	M8 A1	M7 A2	M6 A3	M5 A4	M4 A5	M3 A6	M2 A7	M1 A8	M9 A9	M8 A1	M7 A2
2015	Jan 5	Feb 4	Mar 6	Apr 4	May 5	June 5	July 7	Aug 7	Sept 7	Oct 8	Nov 7	Dec 7
	23:24	13:03	08:47	15:14	10:29	16:20	04:04	16:43	21:44	15:48	21:05	16:11
	Year 4	Year 3	Year 3	Year 3	Year 3	Year 3	Year 3	Year 3	Year 3	Year 3	Year 3	Year 3
	M6 A3	M5 A3	M4 A4	M3 A5	M2 A6	M1 A7	M9 A8	M8 A9	M7 A1	M6 A2	M5 A3	M4 A4
2016	Jan 6	Feb 4	Mar 5	Apr 3	May 4	June 4	July 6	Aug 6	Sept 7	Oct 7	Nov 7	Dec 6
	05:17	18:55	14:34	20:56	16:06	21:55	10:52	22:19	03:23	21:32	02:53	21:48
	Year 3	Year 2	Year 2	Year 2	Year 2	Year 2	Year 2	Year 2	Year 2	Year 2	Year 2	Year 2
	M3 A5	M2 A5	M1 A6	M9 A7	M8 A8	M7 A9	M6 A1	M5 A2	M4 A3	M3 A4	M2 A5	M1 A6
2017	Jan 5	Feb 4	Mar 5	Apr 4	May 4	June 5	July 6	Aug 7	Sept 7	Oct 8	Nov 7	Dec 7
	11:09	00:33	20:22	03:07	21:42	03:25	16:21	03:48	08:58	03:14	08:42	03:43
	Year 2	Year 1	Year 1	Year 1	Year 1	Year 1	Year 1	Year 1	Year 1	Year 1	Year 1	Year 1
	M9 A7	M8 A7	M7 A8	M6 A9	M5 A1	M4 A2	M3 A3	M2 A4	M1 A5	M9 A6	M8 A7	M7 A8

You are a flexible individual who tends to glide around obstacles in life. You possess great power and can achieve much, but your progress and success tend to go on behind the scenes. You are most effective when your build up your life slowly and move fluidly into new situations.

You need your own space, particularly when you are in a relationship. When you have this freedom and independence, you feel safe in the knowledge that you can return to your partner whenever you want. To others, you can seem secretive but, at the same time, you can be affectionate and very loving. You can also be a worrier and, depending on your upbringing, may harbour deep insecurities.

You have the ability to step back from a situation and consider circumstances objectively. At times, this enables you to have exceptional clarity of thought. This characteristic makes spirituality appealing to you and you may find yourself drifting towards religion, spiritual practices or meditation in later years.

Others often find you very sexually appealing and a high-quality sex life is important to you. A deeply satisfying sexual relationship is more rewarding for you than a plentiful one, and you may revel in the secrecy and mysticism of sex, enjoying a slow but very controlled build-up to any sexual activity.

You are a gifted speaker and good at describing your emotions. You hold people's attention in social situations and often seem very open. In spite of this, you tend to hold back on aspects that form part of your deeper self. You often have objective advice for others and can be the voice of reason. You have original ideas and are not affected by other people's opinions.

Although you can relate to people easily on an emotional level, you have a low tolerance for people who are weak. When you are feeling particularly objective and independent, others may see you as unsympathetic and cold. At times you can be too quick to judge others.

Romantically, you are loving and enjoy sexual activity, although you tend to retain your independence. This makes you seem unable to be totally intimate with your partner. You need to spend time on your own and prefer being in a relationship with someone who is secure enough to allow you freedom. You may experience periods of insecurity in your relationship, during which times you may act rashly and bail out.

Typically, you are easy going, laid back and relaxed. You find it easy to mix socially with a wide range of people from different backgrounds. You approach work in a logical and well-reasoned manner and your objectivity makes you able to provide useful advice for others. However, you often tend to worry about the small things in life.

You are a careful, thoughtful and methodical individual. Success is well within your grasp, thanks to your highly practical approach to life. You also possess a unique ability to continually improve yourself and develop particular skills.

You have a cautious approach to life. This characteristic becomes more pronounced as you get older. The advantage of this is that you are prudent and thoughtful when planning your future and manage to make the most of your successes in earlier years. The risk is that you will shy away from adventure and may allow your life to become stagnant. You can avoid potential boredom by striving to expand on your plans and strategies.

You need the security of a steady family and home life. Your dependent streak means that you find it easier to succeed when you have someone to rely on. You make an excellent team player and are a good homemaker. You often find yourself taking care of other people, even though doing so may not have been your initial intention.

Most satisfied in a long-term, secure relationship, you enjoy great intimacy and affection. However, you are able to switch back into a practical, purposeful mode easily. You enjoy an active sex life and make a satisfying and skillful lover. At times you blunt your ambitions by being too realistic and practical. If this is the case, it would help if you teamed up with a more adventurous person.

You think methodically and can study and understand in great depth. Although you may take time to master a concept, once you have done so, you can explain it in the most understandable manner. Similarly, you communicate your own ideas clearly and effectively.

You have a gentle, caring nature and are generally sympathetic to other people's problems. You are careful, tactful and considerate in your relationships and enjoy a very full and satisfying social life because of your genuine interest in other people's lives.

Romantically, you seek a cosy, warm and settled relationship. You like to be with a partner who is reliable and responsible and expect to be treated with care and consideration. However, you often find yourself attracted to people who are fiery, spontaneous and exciting. You have a tendency to be jealous and insecure when an important relationship becomes threatened. Your friends and acquaintances may accuse you of complaining unnecessarily at times and you are sometimes over-critical of them.

You are cautious, careful and concerned with financial security. Your approach to work is realistic and thorough. You are skilled at making, developing and keeping useful business contacts and have the ability to make friendships that will serve you well in the long-term. You will achieve success by building up an effective team of workers.

You are dynamic and active and can become highly driven the instant your enthusiasm is aroused. This enthusiasm helps you start new projects and you find it extremely satisfying to watch your own ideas being put into practice. However, your impatience to see quick results can mean that you lose interest if things don't happen immediately. There is a risk that you will not see projects through to a profitable conclusion, recharging your enthusiasm by beginning another project instead. If you feel that other people are blocking your progress, you can become irritable and lose your temper.

You can become absorbed in technical activities and enjoy researching in detail. You tend to focus your energy and enjoy being specific and precise. This can lead to missed opportunities as you may lose sight of the big picture. Your quick energy keeps you at the forefront of new trends and movements.

Your ideal partner is someone who is positive, enthusiastic and self-assured. As you tend to be career orientated, you would benefit from someone who can help you progress professionally. Your romantic relationships tends to be active ones that are based on doing things together. You do not easily tolerate other people who cannot keep up with your pace.

You are likely to be direct and decisive and enjoy expressing your opinions. Some people may find this frankness a little too abrasive.

Quick to learn new subjects, you easily master technical details. Being accurate and precise is important to you, so you tend to see things in black and white. This gives you the ability to organise your mind so that you store and access information quickly. You have an excellent memory and are quick at producing solutions, both for yourself and for others. Situations that are unclear make you feel uncomfortable, as do people whose minds do not work in a logical fashion.

You are confident and, when confronted with difficulties, remain solution-orientated. You may be rather highly strung and sensitive, which can make you unpredictable.

In romance, you are positive, but your ideal partner needs to be able to tolerate your mood swings and live up to your standards of accuracy.

You are enthusiastic and interested in almost everything. A positive attitude means you quickly attract attention and people are naturally drawn to you.

Starting new projects gives you much enjoyment, but, if unchecked, you can spend too much time setting them up without actually realising the benefits of any. You like to keep busy.

You have a strong desire to progress and enjoy constantly moving into new situations. You like to travel and enjoy working in a variety of countries or visiting exotic, distant places on holiday. When faced with difficulties, you can be tempted to resolve them by moving away and starting again.

You have big ideas and think in global terms. You need to spread your ideas across society, either through your profession or through a hobby such as writing, film, music or photography – all areas in which you should naturally succeed.

There is a gentler side to your character, which can make you shy away from confrontation. This also makes you particularly upset by criticism, so much so that if things go wrong you will sometimes resign yourself to failure and act the victim. At the same time, you have a tenacious streak that can help you keep working towards a goal over a long period of time. However, this can also mean that you carry on with something that has been futile for far too long.

In relationships you tend to be drawn to people who will appreciate your sensitive side and enjoy looking at the big picture in life. Warm, positive and enthusiastic people tend to capture your heart.

You are a highly imaginative person and have an active mind. You are also very creative and can generate new ideas quickly. This means you can walk into any situation and succeed by thinking on your feet. Yet, your ability to think about more than one thing at a time can make it hard for others to hold your attention.

You tend to spend too much time analysing problems when actions would be more appropriate. As a result, you often leave decisions to the last minute. This can be difficult for your colleagues who may find it impossible to know what is going on without concrete planning – to them you seem vague and indecisive.

In relationships you are gentle, sensitive, kind and thoughtful, but also have a ruthless, determined streak. At times you can combine these characteristics to get your own way without anyone realising what has happened. You tend to be drawn to someone who is warm, optimistic and praises your strengths.

You are a gentle, kind and thoughtful individual. People feel relaxed around you and you find it easy to make friends. You are clever and can produce creative and imaginative ideas at work. You can also be very persistent, determined and tenacious when it comes to developing your career.

You possess enormous power to make radical changes in life. This enables you to begin new projects or take on new philosophies with great fervour. The effort you exert in making these changes means that you will stick with your new lifestyle for some time.

You have a desire to take other people with you in your success and, in extreme circumstances, can attempt to convert your friends and family. You may become particularly enthusiastic about one person and build them up to be a hero, only to shift your allegiance when someone new appears on the scene.

You like having people around you and enjoy being the centre of attention. You are happy in a large family, with a wide circle of friends or in a job working with other people. You are socially aware and can understand complex social behaviour within a community.

You can be easily drawn into gossip and often place too great an importance on other people's actions. At times you may be jealous and critical. Although you can hold a well-balanced view of life, you are prone to extreme opinions and strong morals. You are sometimes argumentative, in which case it is important to remember that in the long term it is better to win over the person rather than the actual argument.

You are usually sympathetic and understanding so people trust you. They may also reveal much of their personal life to you without prompting.

You are powerful and bold, but tend to play down these strengths. You can move effortlessly into situations where you are the focus of attention and, having attained this position, you are happy to rise to the occasion.

You are not afraid of confrontation and enjoy a lively discussion. You are a powerful and persuasive speaker and, if pushed too far, your opponents feel the full force. This adds an intimidating aspect to your character. You have good social skills and many friends. You enjoy being a team player in professional situations.

In relationships, you like to feel in control and can be domineering. If you respect your partner, you can show great loyalty and support. You are able to promote and build up your partner socially to considerable effect.

You can present a strong front and make good first impressions, even though you may not be as confident and powerful inside. This will depend on your other nine ki numbers. You can quickly take control of a situation and will not tolerate people who try to take advantage of you.

Your goal is to proceed through life with dignity and integrity. You lead a well-organised and sometimes carefully planned life. You value honesty, trust and respect, factors which influence many of your decisions. Your outlook is mature and you are happy to take on responsibilities. In some ways, all this can make you too serious and you may appear to others as being authoritative and unapproachable.

You can be hurt by any situation that makes you look foolish. To avoid this you sometimes put a little too much energy into proving you are right. You have a sense of wisdom that is valued by others. You are also highly intuitive, perceptive and have a superb sense of timing. If you have learned to trust these skills, you will find them useful throughout life. However, they can lead you to be naive.

Material wealth, prestige and sex all interest you and can be strong motivational forces, driving you to work harder. You often seek out a mentor and set high standards for your friends and colleagues, which can lead to frequent disappointments. You like to feel in control of your life and this desire can extend to your close friends.

In relationships, you need to find a strong person who can win your respect or who is happy to let you make all the important decisions.

You speak with authority and can easily win respect. You value open and honest communication and find it difficult to forgive someone who has lied to you. You rarely offer opinions without being asked, but your blunt manner can cause offence.

You have a fatherly nature and gravitate towards situations in which you are responsible for others. Your intuition helps you make decisions and plan ahead. Bringing a sense of rhythm to whatever you do, you are conscientious about time.

You live by a strong moral code and expect the same behaviour from others. This can frustrate you and, at times, make you appear self-righteous. You enjoy being in control and are not happy under someone else's leadership unless you have a profound respect for him or her. You find it hard to let go, which may make you seem overbearing to others.

You have a formal and dignified manner. Your opinions are strongly held and you invest a lot of energy into proving your point. You are well organised and have an excellent awareness of timing at work.

However, you feel the weight of responsibility on your shoulders at times and are often accused of taking yourself too seriously.

You have a deep-seated need to acquire material wealth and are good at finding ways to make money. You can also be equally good at spending it. In the long term you will be most satisfied if you can build up your wealth and material assets. This will ensure a happy retirement. It is essential that you are able to focus on a positive end result of a project as this gives you hope and the motivation to move forwards. If this is lost, it is easy for you to become depressed and pessimistic.

You like to do things with style and can be charismatic. You have a youthful attitude to life and like to have fun and play around. This aspect of your character often makes you particularly appealing to young children. To other people, you can sometimes appear too childish and immature.

You usually move towards situations that are comfortable and pleasurable for you. Once you are in such an environment, however, you can easily lose motivation and can sometimes become lazy.

Your desire for pleasure means that you enjoy frequent sexual activity. Sex is an important part of a relationship for you and can lead you to devote considerable energy to finding sexual partners.

You are a charming and engaging speaker who is easily motivated by material gain or the opportunity for romance. You enjoy seeing a positive outcome arising from your efforts.

It is important that you feel comfortable, and you prefer easy-going situations. You are sensitive, have a good sense of humour and enjoy the company of people who make you laugh. You normally have a positive and joyful attitude but can sometimes sink into depression. When you are feeling low, you often seek out short-term pleasures or set your sights on an exciting new challenge.

You love attention and adore being pampered. Your ideal partner needs to be pleasure orientated, fun and sensual.

You are fun, entertaining and charming. You are motivated by money and are clever at finding ways to increase your income.

It is hard for you to maintain your drive if your job is boring or does not hold the opportunity for financial improvement. For success, you need to enjoy your work environment.

You are highly competitive and very motivated. There is a danger that you will allow this competitive spirit to take over your life – you may become a workaholic. You are a natural organiser and have the wherewithal to drive your way to the top of your profession.

You are quick to spot opportunities and seize them. You have the courage to make sudden and unpredictable changes to your life.

You are outgoing and enjoy an active and wide-ranging social life. Your quick-wittedness enables you to take the lead comfortably in conversations. You also have a playful streak, which brings out a particularly attractive childlike quality and makes you fun to be around. You do not suffer fools gladly, however, and can sometimes be ruthlessly critical of those who expose any weaknesses.

In a relationship, you bring excitement, drama and activity but, in return, you expect a lot. Your partner may find you slightly spoilt and too ready to let others do things for you. A particularly generous partner may eventually feel taken advantage of.

You are a charismatic speaker and are able to capture an audience's attention. Your clever storytelling keeps others amused. Gregarious, outgoing and sociable, you have a sharp intellect and are knowledgeable on a wide range of subjects.

You are clear-headed, perceptive and insightful. Flashes of intuition restore your faith in the future. You are able to calculate how you will best succeed in any situation and this skill, combined with a competitive streak, often means that you find ways to turn situations to your advantage. Beware, though: to others, this can sometimes look like greediness and they may feel they are being used.

Romantically, you know how to make your partner feel good and can take him or her to highs of excitement. But you also have the ability to bring him or her down again with a few piercing words of criticism.

You tend to be highly strung and, although you can be rough with others at times, you are not good at accepting similar treatment. In fact, attack is often your favourite form of defence.

You are fun, exciting and have a childish sparkle to your character. You are outgoing and inquisitive, and can be disarmingly direct. You are quick to seize opportunities in business and, driven by goals, you like to get on with the job in hand.

NINE KI YEAR NUMBER · 9

Your energy levels, enthusiasm and decisions are often very much emotionally based. Your feelings are easily affected by your friends, colleagues and family. Certain people have the ability to fill you with fire and passion, but this can evaporate quickly. Finding a mentor will help fuel your desires to achieve more in life. On the other hand, some individuals dampen and drain your energy.

You are naturally outgoing and find it easy to meet new people and forge relationships. You are easily noticed in social situations and have the ability to make friends that can later be influential in your career. You have a gift for promoting yourself.

You are energetic, passionate and proud. This makes you an exciting and spontaneous lover, although you can be unpredictable. At times, your partner may find you irrational and over-emotional and you can also be accused of being hard to pin down.

NINE KI MONTH NUMBER · 9

You are a warm, passionate person and are able to convey your emotions eloquently. You are vivacious, friendly and lively.

You are incisive and like to lead discussions. When you get a little over-excited, you tend to monopolise the conversation, but as you are an entertaining speaker, you usually get away with it. At times, you may talk about yourself too much and neglect to show interest in your friends.

You can be fiery and impulsive. These qualities give you a sparkle that makes you stand out in a crowd. In a rush of enthusiasm, you are sometimes prone to exaggeration and you may make promises that you cannot possibly keep. Your decisions are often emotionally led. This can cause you to change your mind.

In a relationship, you can be passionate and loving, and you crave these qualities in your partner. At other times, you may be aloof and distant, which can make you seem selfish. You possess an extremely generous nature, however, and when you are in the right mood or with the right person, you will give your all.

NINE KI AXIS NUMBER · 9

You are quick, bright and expressive, but this can initially be masked by shyness. Once you warm to someone, you show your true colours.

In terms of furthering your career you pin your hopes on making useful social connections and you may devote a large proportion of your time and energy to that end.

Feng shui astrology birth charts

part three

While your code of three numbers provides invaluable insights into the different aspects of your character, you will need to look at your birth chart to make a full assessment of your ki energy. You can either construct and interpret your chart yourself, as explained on pages 34–7, or you can simply find your chart on pages 38–73 and read the analysis provided.

reading your birth chart

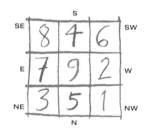

Step 1

Copy down the appropriate birth chart and highlight your month and year numbers. Your year number will strengthen the qualities of the direction in which it is located. If your code is 196 you will have the chart above. Your year number one is in the north-west. In the magic square six occupies this direction.

Constructing your nine ki birth chart is easy. It will look much like the chart on the left, although the numbers may be arranged in a different way. Your nine ki month number is always at the centre of your chart. To find out how the remaining eight numbers are arranged, glance through pages 38–73 and find the chart with your month number at the centre. Each number will occupy a particular position or direction in the chart. To read your chart you will first need to familiarise yourself with the ki energy of each direction (see pages 74–93). Remember that the directions of the feng shui compass are different to the standard compass directions, with north at the bottom of the chart (see page 12). There are six steps to interpreting your birth chart and they are as follows:

Step 1: Locate your nine ki year number

The first step to reading your birth chart is to consider the position of your nine ki year number. The direction in which it falls will give this area of your chart increased activity and ki energy flow. For example, if you have 196 as your nine ki code of numbers, your year number is in the north-west of your chart and this activates the ki energy of the whole axis from the north-west to the south-east. In this case, dignity, honesty and integrity – all qualities associated with the north-west – are connected to the south-east, which is associated with communication. You therefore value honesty, integrity and respect when talking, writing or using other forms of communication. You find it difficult to cope if proved wrong, feeling a loss of dignity. For this reason, you may go to great lengths to prove yourself right and can seem self-righteous.

Step 2: Assess the ki energies of each number

Next, you need to look at where each number falls on the chart. The art of reading a birth chart depends on being able to interpret how the energies of each number and the position it occupies will interact with each other. To do this, you need to familiarise yourself with the attributes of each number and direction as described on pages 74–93.

Because the number five is normally the central number (that is, it occupies the centre in the magic square), it will have a special influence on your chart. You should therefore start with five when you compare the ki energies of the numbers and directions. From the number five, move clockwise around the square as you repeat this analysis for each of the other seven numbers. Taking the same code of 196, the number two occupies the western direction of the chart. The west is associated with romance while two is associated with quality, caution and being practical. Therefore, if your code of numbers is 196, you are slow to start a serious relationship but tend to concentrate your efforts on improving the quality of it in the long-term.

Step 3: Assess the elements

Another step in reading your birth chart relies on knowledge of the principles of the five elements, that is, water, tree, fire, soil and metal (see page 10). You will remember how some elements are harmonious with each other and others are disharmonious, and that each number and each direction is associated with one of the five elements. You now need to consider the interaction between the elements associated with each number on your chart and the direction it occupies. Taking the same example of 196 as your nine ki code of numbers, start with the number five and assess whether the element associated with it (soil) is compatible with that of the north (water). Continue with all the other numbers around the chart in a clockwise direction. Energies that are supportive, such as metal and water, will create a more harmonious flow of ki energy than those that are more destructive such as soil and water.

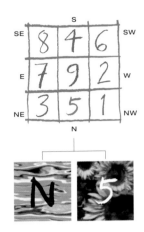

Step 2

Starting with number five, locate its direction on your chart and assess the energy of the direction. For the code 196 five is in the north, so the attributes of the north (water ki energy) will be activated. Continue assessing the ki energies of all the other numbers on your chart.

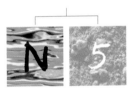

Step 3

Compare the element associated with each number with the element associated with the direction in which it sits. In this example, the soil ki energy of the number five is disharmonious with the water ki energy of the north, which in practice would make it hard for someone with this chart to balance independence and intimacy.

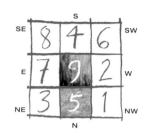

Step 4

Assess whether the element associated with each number is compatible or not with the element associated with the central number. In this example, the fire ki energy of number nine at the centre is in harmony with the soil ki energy of number five, making it easier to move spontaneously into sexual situations or exude sex appeal.

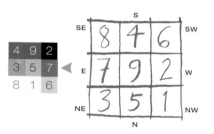

Step 5

Compare your birth chart with the magic square and highlight the number opposite its normal position. If your month number is nine and you have the birth chart above, you will find that seven is opposite its normal position in the magic square. In this case, you are more likely to have unrealistic ambitions concerning wealth and romance, possibly leading to disappointment and frustration.

Step 4: Analyse the ki energy flow along each axis

The next step is to observe how easily ki energy moves along each axis of the chart. If it has to change from one element to another it will slow the flow, whereas adjoining numbers along an axis that has the same element or elements that are harmonious with each other means that ki energy will flow more quickly. This has only a subtle influence on your reading, but can tell you what aspect of your chart you are most comfortable with. To do this you need to look at how the element associated with each of the peripheral eight numbers will interact with the element associated with the central number.

Step 5: Compare your chart to the magic square

Another important number to consider when reading your chart is the nine ki number that is opposite its normal position in the standard 'magic square' chart. The qualities associated with this number will be less stable and harder to depend upon, so you should therefore try to avoid finding yourself in a situation where these aspects of your life present a serious problem.

Step 6: Make a note of your month animal

The final factor to consider when reading your birth chart is the Chinese animals relating to the month you were born. For example, if you were born on 20 May, you were born in the month of the snake. Look at the chart opposite to find out which animal relates to which month. The chart on the far right shows the direction related to each animal. Remember, in feng shui astrology, the months start four to nine days after the Western calendar month; refer to the chart on pages 20–24 to find out the starting date of each month and therefore your month animal.

The significance of your month animal is that it adds more ki energy to this part of your chart, effectively strengthening the qualities related to this direction, and also leaves a slight deficiency of ki energy in the opposite direction.

Special cases

There are some nine ki codes of numbers that have a chart where the year number falls opposite the number five. These codes are 611, 822, 133, 344, 766, 977, 288 and 499. This creates a situation where your year ki number, the energy of which defines your direction and progress in life, is opposite the most powerful ki energy of all the numbers. This can result in your feeling blocked or having difficulty fulfilling your long-term plans. However, the advantage of having one of these nine ki code

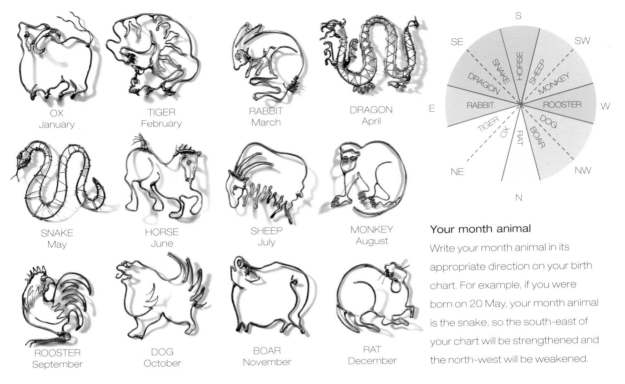

OX
January

TIGER
February

RABBIT
March

DRAGON
April

SNAKE
May

HORSE
June

SHEEP
July

MONKEY
August

ROOSTER
September

DOG
October

BOAR
November

RAT
December

Your month animal

Write your month animal in its appropriate direction on your birth chart. For example, if you were born on 20 May, your month animal is the snake, so the south-east of your chart will be strengthened and the north-west will be weakened.

of numbers is that, at times, you attract help into your life, which is not of your own initiative. If you have one of these codes of numbers, you should be prepared for some unexpected opportunities.

If you have the month number five, your birth chart will be the same as the magic square so your chart will have each of the nine ki energies in its natural position. The more unpredictable and changeable nature of five is balanced by the other numbers and energies being in harmony with each other. Although you may experience strong emotions and changeable opinions as a result, other aspects of your life – such as financial awareness, romance, leadership, planning, organisation, sex, spirituality, motivation, embarking on new projects, communication, creativity, your social and family lives – will all be relatively harmonious. The only thing that can disturb this harmony is the position of the year number and month animal on your chart.

Ready-constructed birth charts

If you don't have time to make and analyse your birth chart, flick through pages 38–73 and find the two pages with your month number top left, which will give you a reading of your chart. The first page provides information covered in steps 1–5; the second page takes a look at the effects of the Chinese animals discussed in step 6.

Step 6

Once you know your month animal, write it in the appropriate direction on your birth chart. For example, if you were born on 20 May, your month animal is the snake, so the south-east of your chart will be strengthened and the north-west will be weakened.

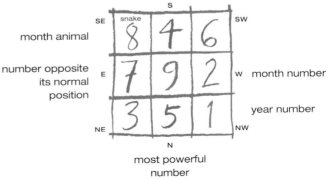

month animal

number opposite its normal position

month number

year number

most powerful number

1 nine ki birth chart

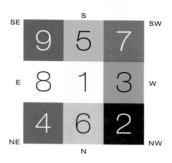

	S	
SE 9	5	7 SW
E 8	1	3 W
NE 4	6	2 NW
	N	

5 Because five is situated in the south, you have a powerful, outward social expression that helps you get noticed, and you usually have a powerful ability to attract people to you. At times, your social relationships can become confrontational, with the risk of upsets and disputes. Five is a ki energy that is changeable so you may find that your feelings towards your social life and friends change easily. This can lead you to withdraw from social life at times.

The water element of one (the number at the centre) can destroy the soil ki energy of five, which can make you feel slightly awkward when first meeting someone. The soil ki energy of five is compatible with the fire ki energy of the south, so you can be effective at expressing emotion. Because of the changeable nature of five, you can experience emotional highs and lows.

3 To the west is number three. This number is associated with activity, ambition and putting ideas into action, whereas the west is associated with romance, financial awareness and pleasure. This combination encourages a very direct approach to romance and money making. You can be very effective at producing futuristic ideas, then putting them into practice profitably.

As three is opposite its normal eastern position in the magic square, you may pursue money and romance too aggressively. Because three has a focussed energy, you will often have a set vision of a lover. This makes it hard to keep an open mind about relationships with other types of people. The ki energy of tree is harmonious with water ki energy at the centre, but not with metal ki energy of the west. This means you may rush into relationships but find them harder to maintain.

7 Moving clockwise finds seven in the south-west. This number is associated with pleasure, romance and contentment, whereas the south-west is associated with family, motherhood and friendships. You therefore approach family life and friendships with a playful sense of fun and can have romantic ideals about them. These aspects of your life can also be a great source of pleasure.

As the south-west relates to the mother, it's likely that you have a pleasurable relationship with your mother. Ideally, she would have provided you with a sense of fun, encouraging your playfulness. If this was the case, you may be looking for such qualities in a lover – someone who is not too serious and who can satisfy your desire for pleasure. Seven is harmonious with both water in the centre and soil in the south-west, making these comfortable aspects of your character.

2 Two occupies the north-west position of your chart. This direction is associated with leadership, organisation and planning ahead, whereas two is associated with being careful, practical and realistic. This combination gives you an ability to lead by building up good relationships and showing you care about those working for you. Conversely, you can build up good relationships with a mentor or with someone you work for. You tend to be cautious when planning ahead and think through all the options carefully before making a decision. As the north-west relates to the father, it is possible that you have a caring relationship with him and feel supported and protected in times of crisis.

The soil ki energy of two is not harmonious with water ki energy in the centre, but it is with metal ki energy of the north-west. This can lead to initial difficulties but long-term success.

6 The northern position of your chart is occupied by six. This direction is associated with sex, self development and spirituality, and the number six relates to being organised, dignified and respected. This means that you prefer to feel in control when initiating sex and tend to take a more dominant role in bed. However, as this direction of your chart is opposite the most powerful ki energy of number five in the south, you may feel that your long-term progress is blocked at times. You can be particularly intuitive about spirituality and religion, and have interesting insights into these matters. You are also able to exert self discipline when it comes to looking after your health, although, again, you might experience times when you feel your efforts are being blocked. The metal ki energy of six mixes harmoniously with the water ki energy of one, which is the central number of your chart. This means that you find matters relating to independence, sex and spirituality comfortable and easy to deal with.

4 Nine ki number four occupies the north-eastern position of your birth chart. This direction is associated with motivation, hard work and competition, while the number four relates to being imaginative, persistent and creative. This means that you tend to be self-motivated and hard working. Any activity that involves communication will be a particularly motivating force for you. You often find imaginative and creative ways of working and can be persistent and tenacious when you find yourself in a competitive situation. Success and wealth will come from hard work and taking opportunities.

The element related to number four is the tree. This ki energy is harmonious with water ki energy, the element related to number one at the centre of your chart. This means that you find it easy to move into a hard-working mode. However, as tree is not harmonious with the soil ki energy associated with the north-east, you may not always find it so easy to maintain such an industrious level of activity.

8 The eastern position is taken by the ki energy of eight. This direction is associated with activity, ambition and putting ideas into action. The number eight relates to being motivated, quick and competitive. You therefore tend to be very motivated and enthusiastic about starting new projects, often rushing into new enterprises. However, there is a risk that you may get bored with these ventures once they are up and running and your attention may wander onto the next plan before you have completed the first.

Soil, the element related to number eight, is not harmonious with water ki energy, the element related to the central number on your chart, or the tree ki energy of the east. This increases the risk that your ambitions turn out to be unrealistic or bring results that you had not originally envisioned.

9 The south-east position of your chart is occupied by the number nine. This direction is associated with communication, creativity and imagination and the number nine is associated with being emotional, expressive and passionate. This gives you the ability to communicate with passion and emotion, and your way of communicating can deeply affect others. You also communicate in a style that gets noticed and draws attention to your ideas.

The fire ki energy associated with number nine is not harmonious with the central water ki energy of one, but it is harmonious with the tree ki energy of the south-east. This means that it may be harder to become creative or use your imagination. However, once you have found something that does inspire you, you will find untapped resources of creativity.

nine ki birth chart

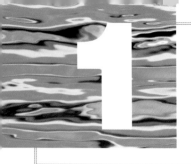

1 1 5

rooster

Because your nine ki year number is in the centre of your chart, all the aspects of your emotional characteristics, as described on page 25, will be more pronounced.

The month ki energy of the rooster increases the western aspects of your chart. Because the west relates to romance, financial awareness and pleasure, you are likely to be successful in these areas or place more importance on them. As ki energy of the east is weaker, you could be less confident and forceful about making changes to your life or starting new things.

2 1 6

rabbit or rat

You have increased ki energy in the north-west of your chart, which makes you appear more dignified, authoritarian and self disciplined. This ki energy also gives you greater desire and strength to reach a leadership position. You can communicate your ideas clearly and logically so that others find them easy to follow.

If you have the month ki energy of the rabbit, you have increased energy in the east. This means you are ambitious, confident and can go out and make things happen. However, you may find it more difficult to complete tasks and partners could find you unromantic.

If you have the month ki energy of the rat, you have greater ki energy in the north of your chart. This can give you greater objectivity, independence and sexuality. As the ki energy of the south is decreased you may find you are less sociable, self-expressive or passionate.

3 1 7

horse

Your year number is to the west of your chart, so you have great financial awareness and can be particularly romantic. You are also ambitious and can make things happen in life.

The ki energy of the horse increases the fiery ki energy of the south. This means you are sociable and easily noticed. You feel things passionately and appear warm to others. The ki energy of the north is decreased, however, so you find it harder to be independent and objective. You may have difficulty overcoming illness.

4 1 8

rooster

Your year number is in the north-east, so you tend to be motivated and can quickly seize an opportunity. You can also be careful, practical and realistic.

The month ki energy of the rooster increases western ki energy, which relates to romance, financial awareness and pleasure. You may be capable in these areas and place great importance on them. As there is less energy in the east you are likely to be cautious about making changes to your life or exploring new avenues.

5 1 9

rabbit or rat

As your year number is situated in the south, this increases the ki energy associated with being flamboyant, outgoing and expressive. You are a passionate individual, but also independent and objective. If you have the month ki energy

of the rabbit, the ki energy in the east of your chart is enhanced. This means you are ambitious and can start up new projects easily. Because western energy is decreased, however, you may not be able to complete tasks and you will not be particularly romantic.

If you have the month ki energy of the rat, you have greater ki energy in the north. This means you are more objective, independent and sexual. This whole north-south axis becomes highly influential in your chart.

horse

Your year number is opposite five, so there is a greater flow of energy along the south-north axis. You are independent, objective and sexual (characteristics of the north), and sociable, expressive and emotional (characteristics of the south). However, the southern aspects of your chart may be harder to control.

The ki energy of the horse increases the southern aspect of your chart even further, making this a highly influential axis in your chart.

rooster

Your year number is in the south-west of your chart, increasing the ki energy in this area. This means you tend to be more cautious, careful and realistic, whilst enjoying long-term friendships. This characteristic becomes stronger in later years. In addition, you are hard-working, competitive and motivated, and able to rise to a challenge.

The month ki energy of the rooster increases the western aspect of your chart, that is, matters relating to romance, financial awareness and pleasure. If such matters are important to you, you are likely to have a talent for them. As eastern ki energy is weakened, you are more cautious about change or trying anything new.

rabbit or rat

Your year number is to the east of your chart, increasing the flow of ki energy in this area. This means you are ambitious, can generate enthusiasm and find it easy to start new projects. Furthermore, you are able to keep an eye on the end result of the project at hand. You also enjoy the pleasures of life and have strong romantic feelings.

If you have the month ki energy of the rabbit, you have an even greater increase of ki energy in the east, making you highly enthusiastic and eager to begin new activities. But decreased energy in the west means that you may not be as good at completing tasks. The strength of your romantic side may also be decreased.

If you have the month ki energy of the rat you have more ki energy of the north. You are therefore objective, independent and sexual. You may not be very sociable or passionate, however, and at times others may even find you rather withdrawn.

horse

Your nine ki year number is in the south-east, which means you tend to be imaginative, creative and persistent. You also have great dignity, are generally well organised and can plan ahead efficiently.

The month ki energy of the horse increases the southern aspect of your chart. This enhances your ability to express yourself, be sociable and get yourself noticed. You feel passionate about things and others see you as a warm person. At the same time, you may find it hard to be independent, objective or overcome illness.

2 nine ki birth chart

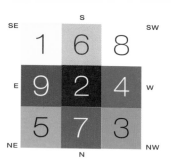

5 Number five is situated in the north-east. This means that you are hard working, especially if you are in a competitive situation or working towards goals. As the north-east ki energy is quick, sharp and piercing you can make sudden, powerful changes in your life. However, you can also use this energy to continue on through difficult times. Because five has a changeable quality, you can find your feelings towards work fluctuating, leading you to explore different options. You have a powerful ability to attract people to work with you, but working relationships can be hard to maintain in the long term and some may end with bad feelings. There may be less stability between work and family life, although they are closely intertwined. The soil ki energy of five is harmonious with the soil ki energies of both the north-east and the number two at the centre of your chart.

9 Moving clockwise to the east of the chart finds nine in this direction. This number is associated with being fiery, expressive and emotional, while the east is associated with ambition, activity and putting ideas into practice. As a result, you tend to approach your career and working life in a way that helps you build up your reputation, increasing the possibility of you becoming a well-known figure. You would also have a fiery approach to the way you do things and feel emotionally attached to your work. This can result in you being somewhat disorganised and chaotic.

The fire ki energy of nine is harmonious with both the soil ki energy of two, your central number, and the tree ki energy of four that is positioned in the east of the magic square. This makes it easy for you to become active and busy, and feel comfortable maintaining such a lifestyle.

1 To the south-east of your chart is the number one. One is associated with being independent, objective and sexual, whereas the south-east is associated with communication, creativity and persistence. This means you have an appreciation of painting, music and books and are often talented in one of these arts. You also have a fluid style of communication. This combination can lead you to move easily into an educational role such as teaching or training. At times, though, you may feel nervous and shy, finding it hard to speak.

The water ki energy of one is not compatible with the soil ki energy of two, the central number in your birth chart, but it is harmonious with the tree energy of the south-east. This means you may need time to talk comfortably with someone, but, once you get to know them, you are able to converse more naturally and fluidly.

6 The southern position of your chart is occupied by the number six. This direction is associated with self expression, emotions and being noticed, whereas the number six is associated with being organised, dignified and in control. You therefore have a tendency to want to control the way people perceive you and are concerned about protecting your reputation and preserving your dignity. You are well organised in situations where you need to present yourself to people and can carry this off in a dignified, graceful manner.

The metal ki energy of six is not harmonious with the fire ki energy of the south, but is compatible with the soil ki energy of two at the centre of your chart. This means you receive public recognition but may not want to sustain it. You may swing from being social, emotional and noticed, to being independent and objective.

Eight occupies the south-west. This direction is associated with family, motherhood and friendships, whereas eight relates to being motivated, quick and competitive. This means you are outgoing when meeting people and making new friends, and are motivated by your family. You also tend to have clear, insightful ideas about raising a family. The position of eight in your birth chart is opposite its normal position in the magic square which can lead to situations where you think you are doing the right thing for friends, family or clients, but it is not actually what those people want. This can cause disappointment and resentment.

Eight is diagonally opposite five, which can make you feel blocked at times by your mother, friends and family. You may fight with your mother and find her both motivating and pushy. Although you might appreciate this in later years, you will tend to resent it at the time.

The soil ki energy of eight is harmonious with both the south-west and two at the centre.

The number four occupies the western direction in your chart. This direction is associated with romance, financial awareness and pleasure, while the number four relates to being imaginative, persistent and creative. This means that you can be persistent and tenacious when pursuing someone to partner you in a romantic relationship, and you will find imaginative and creative ways of raising finance. Although you tend to work at building up your finances to a healthy level, you can easily waste them on impulse or rash ideas. Similarly, there is a risk that you jeopardise a relationship through an ill-thought out action.

Four has the ki energy of tree, which is not harmonious with the soil ki energy two, the number occupying the centre of your birth chart. Nor is four compatible with metal ki energy associated with the west. This can make it harder to maintain a harmonious romantic relationship. You may also find it harder to set up projects that provide a long-term income.

The north-western position is occupied by number three. This direction is associated with leadership, organisation and dignity, while three relates to being active, ambitious and focussed. You are therefore single-minded and ambitious in leadership situations, but can be too frank to cultivate long-term relationships with colleagues. You have good forward-thinking ideas and can inspire people to move into new positions. The north-west relates to the father so your father plays an influential role in your life, instilling you with enthusiasm, ambition and drive, but it may not necessarily be an easy relationship.

The tree ki energy of three isn't harmonious with either the central soil energy of two or the metal ki energy of the north-west. This can make leadership positions uncomfortable.

Seven occupies the northern position of your chart. This direction is associated with sex, spirituality and independence, whereas the number seven is associated with pleasure, fun and romance. This can make sex an important (in some cases the only) source of pleasure for you, which could mean that you come to depend quite heavily on your sexual partner. You also derive great satisfaction from spiritual activities, which can lead to a greater sense of contentment. You also know how to enjoy yourself when you are on your own.

The metal ki energy of seven is compatible with both the water ki energy of the north and the soil ki energy of two at the centre of your chart. This makes it easier for you to move into spiritual or new sexual activities and feel comfortable with these in the long term.

1 2 4

monkey

Your nine ki year number is in the south-east, so you are creative, imaginative and, as long as you have time to plan ahead, can communicate effectively. You also are well-organised, command respect and have natural intuition.

The month ki energy of the monkey increases south-western ki energy. You therefore have a natural ability to form long-term relationships and value those with friends, family and colleagues, especially in times of difficulty. However, you might have periods when you lack motivation and lose your desire to work.

3 2 6

snake

Your year number is in the north-west so you are dignified, appear authoritative and generally need to be in control. You are also creative and communicative.

The month ki energy of the snake increases the energy of south-east, so your imagination is further stimulated and you are keen to spread your new ideas. You also tend to be ideologically orientated. This axis becomes more influential in your chart, putting greater emphasis on relationships and communication.

2 2 5

tiger or boar

Your nine ki year number is at the centre of your chart, so all aspects of your character as defined on page 26 are enhanced. You are able to form long-term relationships with friends, colleagues, business contacts and clients.

If you have the month ki energy of the tiger, you have increased energy in the north-east so you are motivated, competitive and have good business sense. Because the ki energy of the south-west is weakened, you may be less inclined to devote time to family and friends and you may also have an occasional reckless streak.

If you have the month ki energy of the boar you have more north-western ki energy. This means you are more dignified and organised, and others may view you as a natural leader. However, you might feel that you are less sociable or communicative, and prefer to sit back and observe others.

4 2 7

monkey

Your nine ki year number is situated in the west so you tend to be romantic, playful and a lover of life's pleasures. In addition, you are an ambitious individual who is active and keen to make things happen.

The month ki energy of the monkey increases your south-western ki energy. You therefore devote a lot of time and energy to the home, family, and friendships. Because the ki energy of the north-east is weakened, you might feel less motivated about working at times .

5 2 8

tiger or boar

Your year number is in the north-east, so you are quick, competitive, motivated and like challenges. You enjoy friendships, taking care of your family and creating a warm, comfortable home.

If you have the month ki energy of the tiger, north-eastern energy will be exceptionally strong, but hard to control. Therefore, you may be very competitive, but you tend to make sudden changes. You may also be impractical and reckless with money.

If you have the month ki energy of the boar, you have more north-western energy so you are dignified, well organised and have leadership potential. You are often happy just to listen and observe without communicating.

6 2 9

snake

Your nine ki year number is in the south so you are sociable, expressive and emotional, but these characteristics may be hard to control. You are also independent, objective and sexual. Your desire for sex can create gossip which may be harmful to you.

The ki energy of the snake increases south-eastern energy, which means you communicate your ideas effectively and tend to be persistent. Weakened north-western energy means you can be tardy and disorganised.

7 2 1

monkey

Your nine ki year number is in the north of your chart so you tend to be sexual, sociable, expressive and independent. You may become spiritual in later years. Your desire for sex can result in complicated and regrettable situations, which you may be tempted to run away from without resolving.

The month ki energy of the monkey increases the ki energy in the south-west. This means that matters concerning friendship, family and the home are important to you. Because the ki energy of the north-east is not as strong in your chart, you might find that you experience periods when you lack motivation and just drift aimlessly.

8 2 2

tiger or boar

Your year number is in the south-west, opposite number five, so you should let things come to you, rather than going out and trying to make them happen. If you are patient, you can form long-lasting relationships with clients, friends and family. You are also highly motivated and work hard, sometimes to extremes.

If you have the month ki energy of the tiger, your north-eastern energy is increased. This axis becomes highly influential, having your year number, animal and the powerful energy of five all in one line. You will be highly motivated and find friends and family important.

If you have the month ki energy of the boar, you have more north-western energy. You are organised and find it easy to plan ahead. Your intuitive instincts often turn out to be accurate. You also possess good leadership skills, but you may lack persistence and have a tendency to give in too easily.

9 2 3

snake

Your nine ki year number is to the east, so you are active, ambitious and naturally enthusiastic. You can think through the financial implications of ideas and are able to complete projects successfully. You look for situations where you are able to feel contentment.

The ki energy of the snake increases the ki energy of south-east. This means your ideas are very imaginative and you want to communicate them to others. Because north-western energy is decreased, you may be disorganised and find it hard to be punctual.

nine ki birth chart

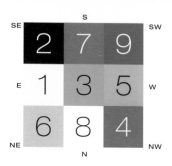

5 Because five is situated in the west, you have a powerful ability to attract romantic partners through big, stylish gestures. As the west is associated with pleasure, you can over indulge in these pursuits at times. Your feelings towards a romantic lover change frequently and when the ki energy of five inevitably changes, you may lose interest. You also have a powerful ability to find ways of making money and can work through to the end of a project, although you may keep changing your mind on how best to do this along the way. With such a strong ki energy in the west, it's not easy for you to relax and feel content.

The soil ki energy of five is compatible with the metal ki energy of the west, but not the tree ki energy of three, your central number. This means you may at first feel awkward moving into romantic situations, but in time feel more comfortable.

4 Moving clockwise to the north-west finds four in this position. Four is associated with being persistent and imaginative, while the north-west is associated with leadership, organisation and dignity. As four is opposite its normal position in the magic square, these areas may not always be harmonious. You may lead and inspire with your ideas and abilities, for example, but not be effective at delegating. You may think your instructions are clear but others may understand them differently. The north-west relates to the father so you might have a good relationship with him, but again, there may be misunderstandings.

The tree ki energy of four is not harmonious with the metal ki energy of the north-west, but it is with tree ki energy of three, your central number. This means you may move into leadership roles quickly, but not enjoy them in the long term.

8 To the north of your chart is the number eight. This number is associated with being competitive, direct and quick, whereas the north is associated with independence, sex and spirituality. This interaction of energies gives you a more direct and aggressive stance when protecting your independence and can also encourage you to be very direct in terms of initiating sex. The playful and boisterous energy associated with the number eight can make you a stimulating lover. You might also have great spiritual insights, although you can find it hard to trust these feelings and let go of the real world in which you operate.

The soil ki energy of eight is not compatible with the water ki energy of the north or the tree ki energy of three at the centre of your chart. This means you may not feel so comfortable exploring the spiritual part of your character.

6 The north-eastern position of your chart is occupied by the number six. This number is associated with being organised, dignified and in control of matters, whereas the north-east is related to self motivation, hard work and winning. This combination means you have the ability to be highly organised when pursuing your goals. You can win with dignity and command respect for your quick and direct approach. You are also capable of working for long periods and are motivated by reaching a position of responsibility or a leadership role.

The metal ki energy of six is harmonious with the soil ki energy of the north-east, but not with the tree ki energy of three at the centre of your chart. This makes it harder for you to move into a hard-working situation, but easier to maintain it once you have arrived there.

1 The number one occupies the eastern position of your chart. This direction is associated with ambition, building up your life and making things happen, whereas one relates to being independent, objective and flexible. This means that you are able to develop your career independently and can start up new projects or businesses by yourself. You can go far in any chosen career if you stay on the right path, but you can also easily change from one job to the next. If the timing is right you can jump higher up the ladder with each change. It is easy for you to take an objective approach to your career to decide in which direction you want to go. As one is opposite the powerful ki energy of five, you may find that all does not go smoothly at times and you meet unexpected obstacles.

The water ki energy of one is in harmony with both the tree energies of the east and three, the number at the centre of your chart. This means that you find it easy to start things and build up your life in the long term.

2 The ki energy of number two occupies the south-eastern direction in your chart. The south-east is associated with communication, imagination and creativity, while the number two relates to being careful, realistic and developing skills through practice. This combination means that you are able to develop the creative side of your character through practice and carefully refining your skills. Rather than allowing your imagination to run wild, you tend to bring your thoughts down to earth by having a strong, realistic approach. As a result, you find it more satisfying to generate creative ideas that can be put into practice realistically. Although frank and to the point, you tend to be cautious when communicating.

The soil ki energy relating to number two is not harmonious with the tree ki energy of the south-east or the tree ki energy at the centre or your chart. This can mean you find it difficult when faced with situations where you are required to be creative or imaginative.

7 The southern position is occupied by the ki energy of seven. The south relates to emotions, being noticed and a social life, while seven relates to being charming, stylish and charismatic. You therefore tend to develop a good social life through your ability to be charming and have fun. However, you are also sensitive in social situations and can easily take offence or feel upset if you feel that someone has been mistreating you. You may gravitate towards people with good manners and charm.

The metal ki energy of number seven is not harmonious with either the fire ki energy of the south or the tree ki energy of number three at the centre of your chart. This means that you can feel a little uncomfortable in situations where you attract a lot of publicity or attention, or where you have to be sociable.

9 The number nine occupies the south-western position of your chart. This direction is associated with family, friendships and the home, whereas nine is associated with being passionate, emotional and expressive. As a result, you relate to friends and family on an emotional level, especially when things are not going well for you. There is also a risk that you may want to separate from these people in later life because they have hurt you emotionally. As this ki energy relates to the mother you may have a warm relationship with your mother, but at times it can be potentially explosive.

The fire ki energy of nine is compatible with both the soil ki energy of the south-west and the tree ki energy at the centre of your chart. This means you feel content and harmonious in family situations.

3 nine ki birthchart

1 3 3

sheep

Your year number is in the east so you are effective at starting new projects and can focus on the end result. As your year number is opposite five, you will find the most successful strategy in life is to go with the flow rather than to try to create opportunities out of thin air.

The month ki energy of the sheep increases south-western ki energy. This means that friendships, family and colleagues are important to you, especially in times of difficulty, and you form long-term relationships. Because north-eastern energy is decreased, you may lack motivation.

2 3 4

dog

Your year number is in the south-east, which means you are imaginative and enjoy expounding new ideas. You do this with a sense of authority.

The month ki energy of the dog increases north-west energy which gives you dignity, respectability and organisational skills. Others may see you as a natural leader. However, you may not be very communicative and prefer just to sit back and observe people instead.

3 3 5

dragon or ox

Your nine ki year number is the centre of your chart so all of the aspects of your characteristics as defined on page 27 are enhanced. You are very active and can make things happen in your life.

If you have the month ki energy of the dragon, south-eastern energy is increased. This helps you generate and spread new ideas. You are also ideologically orientated. Weakened north-western energy means you find it difficult to plan ahead and organise. You also feel insecure if things are not under your control.

If you have the ki energy of the ox, north-eastern energy is increased in your chart. This makes you motivated, competitive and have a direct approach to life. However, you have less time for friends and family and may not be good at consolidating your gains.

4 3 6

sheep

Your year number is in the north-west, so you tend to appear dignified and are seen as trustworthy and respectable. You are also creative and are keen to communicate your ideas to others.

The month ki energy of the sheep increases south-western energy. This direction is related to friendships, family and the home, so these areas of your life are important to you. However, at times you may feel unmotivated.

5 3 7

dog

Your nine ki year number is situated in the west and this direction is even more pronounced because the powerful ki energy of five is also there. This means that you are a romantic individual who enjoys pursuing pleasure. You are also financially aware. The influence of five creates a risk that you will overspend, however, as it will encourage you to seek amusement to the point of decadence.

The month ki energy of the dog relates to the north-west, so you are organised, dignified, and have leadership potential. You are also happy simply to listen for periods without wanting to communicate.

6 3 8

dragon or ox

Your nine ki year number is in the north-east, so you are competitive, direct and motivated. You are probably good at developing long-term friendships and family relationships. You also have the ability to spot new opportunities and seize them quickly.

If you have the month ki energy of the dragon, you have increased south-eastern energy. This gives you a strong ability to communicate and spread your ideas. You also tend to be persistent. Decreased energy in the north-west makes it hard for you to be organised or punctual.

If you have the month ki energy of the ox, you have increased north-eastern energy. This is also the direction of your year number, so you have a greater capacity to be motivated and succeed at trading or other speculative activities. Your chart is less balanced, however, so you can become obsessive. Overwork may lead to poor health.

7 3 9

sheep

Your nine ki year number is in the south, so you are more likely to be social, expressive and self-promoting. You stand out easily in social situations and take pride in cultivating your reputation. In addition, you are independent and sexual. Sometimes your desire for sex can result in complicated social situations and malicious gossip.

The month ki energy of the sheep increases south-western energy. This means friendships, family and the home are important to you. Because you have decreased energy in the north-east, you may lose motivation at times.

8 3 1

dog

Your year number is in the north of your chart, so this means you have a greater desire to maintain your independence. You tend to be sexual and are often attracted to spiritual philosophies. You enjoy being social, expressing yourself and can easily make an impression.

The month ki energy of the dog enhances the north-western ki energy. This means you have dignity, good organisational skills and leadership potential. You could also be very intuitive. Because there is less energy in the south-east, you may not be particularly persistent and, in consequence, tend to give in too easily at times.

9 3 2

dragon or ox

Your nine ki year number is in the south-west, so you tend to be cautious, realistic and practical. You are likely to find it easy to work hard and enjoy competing with others. You are also good at maintaining long-term friendships and harmonious family relationships.

If you have the month ki energy of the dragon, you have increased south-eastern energy. This increases your ability to have imaginative ideas, which you enjoy communicating to others. Because you have decreased north-western energy, you may find it difficult to be punctual and organised, which can make you feel less in control of situations. This disorganisation and the resulting feelings of lack of control can also harm your sense of dignity.

If you have the month ki energy of the ox, you have increased north-eastern energy. You therefore tend to be motivated and hard working, although this can be at the expense of quality time spent with friends and family. You are also highly intuitive and may often find that you make the right decisions instinctively. This axis will be more influential in your chart.

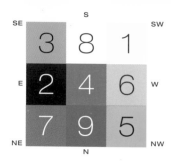

4 nine ki birth chart

5 Number five is situated in the north-west, so you have a powerful ability to attract people who seek your guidance and advise. This helps you build up a dignified image and win people's trust. When the ki energy of five inevitably changes you may temporarily lose interest in other people's problems. As the north-west is associated with control and organisation, you can be authoritarian at times. At other times you may prefer someone else to take responsibility for organising matters. You have a strong leadership potential but may find this hard to maintain in the long term.

The soil ki energy of five is harmonious with the metal ki energy of the north-west, but it is not harmonious with the tree ki energy of four at the centre of your chart. This means you may feel awkward going into a leadership position, but feel more comfortable the longer you are in this role.

9 Moving clockwise, the north position of your chart is occupied by the number nine. Nine is associated with being passionate, emotional and expressive, while the north relates to independence, sex and spirituality. You therefore tend to have a passionate sexual desire and usually make an affectionate lover. However, as nine is opposite its normal position in the magic square, these aspects may not always be harmonious. You may find it hard to combine your desire with independence. This can cause you to switch from one to another as you become dissatisfied with both. The combination of fire and water elements means you have a feel for spiritual matters, but find it hard to explain this in practical terms. The fire ki energy of nine is not harmonious with the water ki energy of the north, making it harder for you to keep up any spiritual practices or health regimes.

7 The number seven occupies the north-east of your chart. Seven is associated with being financially aware, whereas the north-east is associated with self-motivation, hard work and winning. You therefore tend to be stimulated by material wealth and find financial goals motivating. The ki energies of both the north-east and the number seven relate to the youngest members of the family, so you tend to have a playful, youthful and fun approach when it comes to getting what you want. The best strategy for winning is probably by charming your way into other people's good books.

The metal ki energy of seven is harmonious with the soil ki energy of the north-east but not with the tree ki energy of four at the centre of your chart. This makes it harder for you to get working but, once started, you gain stamina and succeed in pacing yourself through a longer task.

2 The number two occupies the eastern position of your chart. This direction is associated with ambition, activity and starting new projects, while two is associated with being dependent, practical and realistic. This means that you can embark on new ventures in a practical and realistic manner, but are likely to find this easier when you work with another person or as part of a team. When you have the support of a close friend you can become more ambitious. You also tend to become more active when you find yourself in the company of someone who is enthusiastic.

The soil ki energy of two is not harmonious with the tree ki energy of the east. This increases the risk of your ambitions and goals not turning out the way you expected them to. It is therefore better that you keep an open mind when thinking about such outcomes.

3 The south-eastern position of your birth chart is occupied by the nine ki energy of number three. The south-east is associated with communication, creativity and persistence, while the number three relates to being ambitious, active and enthusiastic. This means that you get easily fired up about opportunities to communicate or spread your ideas to other people. You tend to have a very active mind, with a highly vivid imagination and a wealth of ideas. You are easily stimulated when involved in creative endeavours such as acting, music, writing or films. As three is opposite the powerful nine ki number five, you may go through periods in your life in which you feel blocked or like you are lacking creativity.

The tree ki energy relating to number three is harmonious with both the tree energy of the south-east and the tree energy of four at the centre of your birth chart. This means that you find the areas relating to these nine ki energies easy and comfortable aspects of your life.

8 The number eight occupies the southern position of your birth chart. This direction is associated with self expression, social life and public recognition, while the number eight is associated with being motivated, competitive and quick. You therefore find that you can seize opportunities quickly to promote yourself and that you tend to compete with others in order to build up your reputation. You can also become jealous if other people are seen to take the credit for matters that you think you should have received recognition for. You are generally outgoing and find it easy to make friends. You tend to have an inquisitive streak in your nature and, on occasions, you can be surprisingly direct with other people.

The soil ki energy of eight isn't harmonious with either the fire ki energy of the south or the tree ki energy of four, the number at the centre of your chart. This means you can find fame and public recognition harder to realise and uncomfortable to live with once you do so.

1 The ki energy of number one occupies the south-western position of your chart. This direction is associated with family life, friendships and the home, while number one relates to being independent, affectionate and objective. This suggests that you have an affectionate relationship with your mother (particularly if you are male), and expect a similar relationship with your lover. At times you may feel isolated from your mother and, if this is the case, you can be nervous of separating from loved ones. You can make friends with people from a wide range of backgrounds and although you can seem distant at times, you are generally very affectionate to family and friends. You are likely to retain your independence and are not easily influenced by friends and family over issues that you hold dear.

6 Six occupies the western position of your chart. This direction is associated with romance, financial awareness and pleasure, while six relates to being organised, in control and dignified. This means that you find money important as it provides you with dignity. You are able to plan ahead and develop a sound, long-term strategy for developing your wealth. You take romantic relationships seriously and need reassurance so that you can proceed without losing dignity. It is not so easy for you to relax and just take each day as it comes.

The metal ki energy of six is harmonious with the metal ki energy of the west, but not with the tree ki energy at the centre of your chart. This means you find it hard to move into romantic or money-making situations but once there, you can easily maintain them.

1 4 2

horse

Your nine ki year number is in the south-west, so you are quick, self-motivated, competitive, cautious and practical. You work best in a team and enjoy long-term friendships.

The month ki energy of the horse increases southern energy, which means you are emotional, social and easily noticed. Others see you as a warm person. Because northern energy is decreased, it's hard for you to be independent, objective or overcome illness.

2 4 3

rooster

Your year number is in the east, so you tend to be ambitious and enthusiastic, especially in terms of material gain and your ideal partner.

The month ki energy of the rooster increases western ki energy so that matters relating to romance and pleasure are important to you. You are also very financially aware. This whole axis becomes more influential in your chart. You find that moving forwards and achieving your goals in life are more important.

3 4 4

rabbit or rat

Your nine ki year number is in the south-east, so you are an effective communicator and express ideas logically. Because your year number is opposite number five, it is more effective for you to wait for things to happen rather than being proactive.

If you have the month ki energy of the rabbit, increased eastern energy makes you ambitious and keen to start new projects. But decreased energy in the west prevents you from completing them as you are easily bored.

If you have the month ki energy of the rat, you have more northern energy, so you're objective and sexual. However, you may not be so social or passionate, and often retreat into your own space.

4 4 5

horse

Your year number is situated in the centre of your chart, so all aspects of your character as described on page 28 are enhanced. You are proactive, creative and keen to communicate your ideas. Others find you trustworthy and you command their respect.

The ki energy of the horse increases southern energy, so you are sociable and easily noticed. You feel things passionately and others view you as a warm person. However, you may find it hard to be independent and objective, and could experience difficulty recuperating from illness.

5 4 6

rooster

Your nine ki year number is in the north-west of your chart, so you naturally gravitate towards leadership positions. You can communicate your ideas with authority and command respect from others.

The month ki energy of the rooster increases ki energy in the west. This is related to romance, financial awareness and pleasure, so these matters are important to you. You may be cautious about activity or starting new projects.

6 4 7

rabbit or rat

Your nine ki year number is in the west, so you are likely to be ambitious and forward thinking. You are good at seeing projects through to a successful conclusion and can build up your life to produce great financial rewards. You also have a romantic streak.

If you have the month ki energy of the rabbit you have increased eastern energy, so you are ambitious and enjoy creating new opportunities. This whole axis will be more active, so you will place greater importance on making things happen and reaping the rewards.

If you have the month ki energy of the rat you have more northern ki energy. This gives you greater objectivity, independence and sexuality. You will also be able to detach yourself from your emotions and look at things objectively. Because you have decreased energy in the south, you may not be very sociable at times and could lack passion.

8 4 9

rooster

Your nine ki year number is to the south of your chart, which means you like being social and getting noticed. In addition to this, you are sexual, independent and individualistic, and often have a generous nature. Others perceive you as being warm and passionate.

The month ki energy of the rooster increases western ki energy, so matters relating to romance, financial awareness and pleasure are important to you. Because eastern energy is weakened, you are cautious about embarking on new ventures or activities.

9 4 1

rabbit or rat

Your nine ki year number is in the north of your birth chart so you tend to be independent, sexual and spiritual, as well as sociable and outgoing. You are also able to switch from being warm, expressive and fiery, to being more objective, withdrawn and clinical.

If you have the month ki energy of the rabbit, you have an increase of ki energy in the east of your birth chart. This means that you are likely to be ambitious and enjoy the chance to go out, start new projects and generally make things happen. However, because you have less western ki energy, you may find it difficult to focus on the end result of a project and to complete tasks fully. You could also find it harder to be romantic.

If you have the month ki energy of the rat, you have more ki energy relating to the north. As a result, you tend to have greater objectivity, independence and sexuality. However, because there is a decrease of southern ki energy in your chart, you may not be very sociable, expressive or passionate about matters.

7 4 8

horse

Your nine ki year number is in the north-east of your chart. As a result, you tend to be more competitive, self motivated and hard working. You are also quick to spot business opportunities and act upon them. You enjoy close friendships with a few people and are happy in a family situation.

The ki energy of the horse increases the fiery ki energy of south. This increases your ability to be social, get noticed and express yourself. You have strong emotions and feel passionately about things. Because the ki energy of the north is decreased, you find it harder to be objective and recover from bad health. You may also feel uncomfortable being on your own, preferring the company of friends.

5 nine ki birth chart

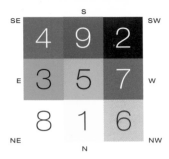

	S	
SE 4	9	2 SW
E 3	5	7 W
NE 8	1	6 NW
	N	

9 The fire ki energy of number nine occupies the south of your birth chart and this is in harmony with the soil ki energy of number five at the centre. This means you find it easy to move into situations where you are highly visible and can enjoy fame, public recognition and an exciting social life. You usually succeed in careers that relate to these aspects of your life.

You could also find your emotions are fiery and change quickly. They are also easily influenced by other people. Individuals that you respect and find inspiring will keep your spirits high and help you through difficult times. Other people can easily damage your pride.

You are someone who takes pride in whatever you do, especially when it comes to your successes. At times you may need to be careful not to offend those who are less successful.

7 To the west of your chart is the metal ki energy of number seven. This ki energy is harmonious with the soil ki energy of number five at the centre of your chart and this means that you can quickly develop strong feelings for someone. Similarly, you are able to move quickly into situations that allow you to make money.

Romantic relationships and material wealth are potentially great sources of pleasure for you. You can use your natural charm to open up new opportunities in these areas of your life. They can also be issues in your life that you feel particularly sensitive about, especially if they do not work out as you had hoped.

You should be able to complete projects to your immense satisfaction and, as a result, will enjoy the feeling of contentment and security later on in life.

2 Moving clockwise to the south-west is number two. The soil ki energy of this number is harmonious with the soil ki energy of number five at the centre. In fact, the whole diagonal axis is made up of numbers that have soil as their ki energy, allowing this energy to wash back and forth easily as it does not have to transform itself into another element. This means that although you are happy in family situations and enjoy friendships, you can be dramatically affected by any upsets. A big argument or dispute with someone close to you can generate waves along this axis that are harder to control and the deep emotions that this evokes can affect all areas of your life.

You will be perceived by others as someone who is caring, sympathetic and motherly, although you can have strong feelings of jealousy. You attract people who need a helping hand.

6 In the north-west position of your chart is the metal ki energy of number six. This ki energy is in harmony with the soil ki energy of five at the centre. This means you find it easy to move into leadership positions and are comfortable taking on responsibilities. As the north-west relates to the father, it should be easy for you to have a harmonious relationship with your father as long as both of you can avoid serious confrontations.

You tend to combine leadership with dignity and want to carry out your responsibilities in a way that commands respect. There is a risk that you will become too dictatorial and exert too much control over the people who are close to you.

You have accurate intuition about people and are a good judge of character. With age, you may develop an admirable air of wisdom which will lead others to seek your advice.

1 The northern position of your chart is occupied by the water ki energy of number one. This is not harmonious with the soil ki energy of five at the centre of your chart and can make you slightly nervous in regard to sex or spirituality. It also means that you worry more in general. Once you have overcome initial reservations, however, you become comfortable and confident about sex and spirituality. More than this, they can actually become powerful forces in your existence.

From time to time, you will feel the need to find a sanctuary into which you can retreat so that you can regenerate yourself, both physically and mentally. As long as you look after yourself in this way, you should be able to maintain good health.

Although you can be confrontational, you do possess a certain amount of flexibility, which you can deploy to avoid difficult obstacles in life. You need to draw out and develop this aspect of your ki energy.

8 The north-eastern direction of your chart is occupied by the soil ki energy of number eight, which is harmonious with five at the centre. In fact, this diagonal axis is made up of numbers that all have soil ki energies, allowing ki energy to wash back and forth easily. This means that although you are naturally self-motivated, you oscillate between being obsessed with your work and lacking motivation or direction in life.

When you have found the right thing for you, you become hard working and dedicated to the project at hand. You can be quick to seize an opportunity and swiftly turn it to your advantage. This aspect of your chart can also lead you to want to organise people and sometimes take over situations. Once you become highly motivated you can be perceived as too pushy and may be accused of seeking to take all the rewards for yourself, even though this is not your intention. At other times, you may drift for a while, being indecisive and unsure of how to move forward.

3 The east of your chart is occupied by the tree ki energy of number three. This does not combine harmoniously with the soil ki energy of number five at the centre of your chart. As a result, you may find it harder to start new projects on your own, preferring to work with a partner or in a team. You may also find that putting your ideas into practice does not always work out as smoothly as expected.

You tend to be ambitious and you can be impatient to make progress on projects, or in life generally. You are excellent at focussing on details and can be very accurate and precise.

You may find that you have to go through a period in which you lack confidence and self-belief before you can cross over into being sufficiently self-assured and motivated to take risks that will make things happen.

4 The south-east of your chart is occupied by the tree ki energy of number four. This energy is not harmonious with the soil ki energy of number five at the centre. This means that you are initially uncomfortable in situations that require you to be creative. However, despite this, you can become an excellent communicator, trainer or artist.

Once you overcome initial reservations, you can be very persistent and tenacious. Although you may need to work at it, you can develop a lively imagination and turn this to creative projects. You may, however, be reluctant to engage in creative pursuits because of your sensitivity to criticism. If you can enlist the support of someone who will encourage you with enthusiasm and a positive attitude, you will find that you will make swift progress.

1 5 1

snake

Your nine ki year number is to the north. As a result, you are independent and enjoy spending time on your own. You can, however, be sociable and expressive. You are also a sexual person, and may explore your more spiritual side later on in life.

The ki energy of the snake increases the ki energy of south-east. This means that you have a desire to share your ideas and fully stimulate and free your imagination. However, you find it hard to plan ahead and can feel insecure if things are not within your control.

2 5 2

monkey

Your nine ki year number is to the south-west. Consequently, you have the ability to form long-lasting relationships with friends, family and clients. You are also able to motivate yourself to work very hard.

The month ki energy of the monkey increases the ki energy in the south-west even further. This means that loved ones are very important to you. Your gossiping, however, may jeopardise your relationships.

3 5 3

tiger or boar

Your nine ki year number is to the east. You are therefore ambitious, confident and dynamic. You are also excellent at organising projects and considering the financial implications of decisions.

The month ki energy of the tiger increases the energy of the north-east. This gives you motivation and great business sense. But you could find you have less ki energy to devote to family and friends.

The month ki energy of the boar gives you greater ki energy in the north-west. This means you are organised, dignified and respectable. At times, you prefer to opt out of conversation and observe.

4 5 4

snake

Your nine ki year number is to the south-east. This strengthens your ability to communicate and activates your creativity. You possess natural intuition and an air of dignity, and also tend to be well organised.

The ki energy of the snake increases south-eastern energy even further. As a result, you can be extremely tenacious and defiant. Creativity, control and organisation are more important to you. If you learn how to let go of things, you will find it easier to move on in life.

5 5 5

monkey

Your nine ki year number is in the centre of your chart. This strengthens the characteristics defined by your month number on page 29. This is the most powerful of all 108 possible combinations – you should use your potent ki energy very wisely to guard against making reckless mistakes or overreacting.

The month ki energy of the monkey increases the aspects of the chart in the south-west that relate to family and friends. Your work may suffer, however, as you may lack drive and purpose.

6 5 6

tiger or boar

Your nine ki year number is to the north-west, which increases the ki energy along this axis. This gives you dignity and increases your need to feel in control. You also have a leaning towards creativity and are able to communicate your ideas.

The month ki energy of the tiger increases the ki energy of the north-east. This strengthens your desire to compete and work hard but also increases the risk of your making unpredictable changes. You may also lack commitment to friends and family, devoting more energy to your work.

The month ki energy of the boar means even greater ki energy relating to the north-west. This gives you increased organisational abilities and leadership potential. At times, though, you are happy to watch and listen to discussions, without wishing to communicate.

7 5 7

snake

Your nine ki year number is situated to the west of your chart, which increases the presence of ki energy along this axis. You are romantic, playful and you enjoy the pleasures in life. Furthermore, you are ambitious, active and keen to go out and make things happen.

The ki energy of the snake increases the energy of the south-east. This enhances your need to stimulate your imagination frequently and means that you are skilled at generating new ideas. You are ideologically minded, but you find it difficult to plan ahead and have a tendency to feel very uneasy if you have to work within a strict structure.

8 5 8

monkey

You experience a great flow of ki energy along the axis running from north-east to south-west. It is more pronounced as the powerful ki energy of five is also there. This increases your competitive edge and means you are keen to take on challenges. You also enjoy home life and spending time with family and friends.

The month ki energy of the monkey increases the aspects of the chart in the south-west relating to friends and family, making this an even more powerful axis. Winning is your great strength.

9 5 9

tiger or boar

You have increased ki energy along the south–north axis of your chart. This means stronger ki energy associated with social life and self expression – you are intelligent and highly entertaining in conversation. As an independent individual who is also highly sexual, there is a slight risk that combining your desire for sex with influential people may result in gossip that could do you some harm.

The ki energy of the tiger increases the energy of the north-east. You enjoy winning, are conscientious, quick-witted and competitive. This natural drive and motivation may mean that you sometimes selfishly neglect your family and friends.

The month ki energy of the boar gives greater ki energy relating to the north-west. This gives you admirable organisational abilities, leadership skills and intelligent forward thinking. Your intuition is often spot on. You have deficient ki energy for qualities such as tenacity and persistence, however, and have a tendency to give in too easily.

nine ki birth chart

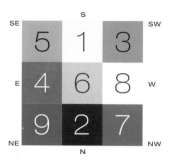

SE	S		SW
5	1	3	
E	4	6	8	W
	9	2	7	
NE	N		NW

5 Number five is situated in the south-east position of your chart, which means you have a powerful desire to communicate and spread your ideas. As the south-east relates to imagination and creativity, you are likely to have interesting and unusual ideas. The ki energy of number five is changeable, so the results of your communication can be unpredictable. You can have great success in putting forward your ideas, but are not always able to repeat this easily. However, you do tend to make an impression on others easily. By communicating your ideas you can attract people to you.

The soil ki energy of number five is harmonious with the ki energy of six, the number central to your chart, but not the tree ki energy of the south-east. This means that although you find it easy to communicate your ideas, you are less comfortable with being creative on a regular basis.

1 Moving clockwise to the southern position of your chart is number one. This number is associated with being independent, sexual and objective, while the south is related to public recognition, self expression and social life. You therefore tend to approach your social life in a style that allows you to interact with people from all different kinds of background. You can also attract attention, although this may take time and it is unlikely that you want to enjoy fame in the long-term. You can usually retain your independence, and your objective approach encourages you to put ideals before friendship. As one is opposite its normal position in the magic square, you have an increased risk of unexpected outcomes in your social life. Water and metal ki energies are harmonious, which makes these aspects of your chart easy to move into but difficult to maintain.

3 To the south-west of your chart is three. This number is associated with being active, ambitious and dynamic, whereas the south-west is related to family, friends and the home. This means you have a direct and active approach to friendships, finding it easy to meet new people and become friends. You may be cautious when starting a family, but enjoy building a home life and may be ambitious in setting standards for the place in which you live. You can find family life frustrating and become impatient or angry with other family members, although this usually blows over quickly. The south-west relates to the mother so your relationship with your mother is probably largely based on doing things together. The tree ki energy of three is not harmonious with the soil ki energy of the south-west, so this can make you feel uncomfortable about these areas of your life.

8 The number eight takes the west position of your chart. This direction is associated with romance, financial awareness and completing projects, whereas eight is associated with being self-motivated, hard working and competitive. This means that you become hard working when motivated by money. You are quick to spot new financial opportunities and can pursue them competitively. You are also quick to begin romantic relationships and can easily move forward in them. However, you may become too preoccupied with accumulating material wealth to enjoy other pleasures in life.

Because the soil energy of number eight is harmonious with the metal ki energy of the centre and west, it is easy for you to settle into situations involving finance and romance. You will find both of these aspects of your life very satisfying in the long term.

7 The north-western position of your chart is occupied by seven. This number is associated with being fun, romantic and content, while the north-west is associated with leadership, organisation and dignity. This means that you prefer to lead by making work enjoyable. You can create a pleasant working environment but retain your dignity at the same time. As the north-west is associated with the father, you seek a relationship with your father where you can feel comfortable joking about and having fun. If you are male, you may wish to have a similar relationship with your own children. However, seven is diagonally opposite the powerful ki energy of number five so it can be hard to make these relationships work out as planned.

The harmonious metal ki energies of the numbers seven and six (the number at the centre of your chart) and the north-west mean that you are comfortable with and can easily attain such qualities as leadership, organisation and dignity.

2 The number two occupies the northern position of your birth chart. This direction is associated with sex, independence and spirituality, while the number two relates to being cautious, practical and realistic. This means that you can be cautious about initiating sex but, over a period of time, can become more comfortable being intimate and have the potential to be a satisfying lover. The more dependent nature of number two can mean that you find solace in sex and rely on your sexual partner during emotional difficulties. In a similar way, you may slowly become attracted to spiritual matters and become more and more dependent on this side of your life in times of crisis.

The soil ki energy of two is harmonious with the metal ki energy of six at the centre of your chart, but not with the water ki energy of the north. This means you find it easy to move into an affectionate relationship with someone, but not to balance the feelings of dependence with the desire to be independent.

9 The north-eastern position is occupied by nine. This direction is associated with motivation, hard work and a competitive streak, while nine relates to being passionate, emotional and expressive. This means that you probably enjoy competitive sports and tend to be passionate about winning. However, the stress and upset of losing could reach such a point that it puts you off competitions altogether.

You are also motivated on a more emotional level, so that if something feels right or the other people involved are stimulating, you find it easy to work hard and succeed. However, you may misjudge a situation and rush into it, later realising that it is not emotionally satisfying. Once you have found the right situation, it is easier for you to stay motivated, work hard and enjoy competition.

4 The ki energy of number four occupies the eastern position of your birth chart. This direction is associated with ambition, activity and starting new projects, while the number four is associated with being imaginative, creative and also persistent. As a result you have the ability to start new things with imagination and generally build up your life easily. You tend to be very active and are particularly good at putting your ideas into action.

The tree ki energy of four is not harmonious with the metal ki energy of six at the centre of your chart, but it is harmonious with the tree ki energy of the east. This may make it harder for you to start something new or be ambitious, but once you are confident in these areas, you can set your sights much higher and will enjoy working towards your goals.

6 nine ki birth chart

1 6 9

dragon or ox

Your nine ki year number is to the south of your chart which means that you are sociable, expressive and outgoing. You are also independent and at times sexual. You have an admirable ability to take clear, objective ideas and express them in a way that adds a more human, emotional touch.

The dragon increases the ki energy of south-east. This strengthens your desire to keep your imagination stimulated and to spread your ideas. You are a persistent person, but you find it difficult to organise things, particularly when it comes to making detailed plans or arrangements.

The ox is to the north-east and increases this ki energy in the chart. This means that you are motivated and competitive, with a direct approach to life. You may have less energy to devote to friends and family and this can lead your loved ones to feel neglected or even that you take advantage of them.

2 6 1

sheep

Your year number is to the north, meaning that you value your independence and often feel the need to spend time on your own. You also delight in the warmth of other people's company, however, and are comfortable and happy in social situations. You are an objective thinker and may find yourself attracted to spiritual philosophies.

The sheep increases the aspects of the chart in the south-west, relating to family, friends and the home – all of which are very important to you. You have a tendency to go through periods when you lack motivation and avoid competitive situations.

3 6 2

dog

Your year number is to the south-west which means that you are cautious, realistic and practical. You are able to work hard over long periods of time. You have the ability to develop skills, and to maintain long-term friendships and harmonious family relationships.

The dog gives you greater energy relating to the north-west. This makes you a highly dignified and organised individual with leadership potential. You may go through periods when you lack inspiration, however, and find it difficult to be creative or imaginative.

4 6 3

dragon or ox

Your nine ki year number is to the east, which strengthens the aspect of your chart relating to ambition and activity. You are the sort of person who will implement an initial idea and see the project through to a successful conclusion. You are also romantic and usually feel content with life.

The ki energy of the dragon increases the ki energy of south-east. This augments your desire to propagate your ideas. You have a great ability to communicate and tend to be persistent. Sometimes, however, you find it difficult to be organised and to manage your day efficiently in terms of time. You are particularly sensitive to any situation in which you feel you could lose dignity.

The ox is to the north-east increasing this ki energy. You are a highly motivated individual and have the potential to excel in trade or in any activity that involves speculation. You thrive on competitive situations and enjoy working towards clearly defined goals.

5 6 4

sheep

Your year number is to the south-east, and because it is the number five, this axis has a powerful influence. You use your imagination to generate ideas which you then seek to realise. You have an organised mind and are able to communicate concepts with a sense of authority.

The sheep increases the aspects of the chart in the south-west, relating to friends, family and colleagues. You have an ability to form successful long-term relationships. You can sometimes lose the desire to work, however, especially if you have been hurt by criticism or have suffered a loss of pride.

6 6 5

dog

Your nine ki year number is in the centre of your chart, strengthening all the aspects of your emotional characteristics as defined by your month number on page 30. You have great strength in leadership and are excellent at organising people.

The dog provides greater ki energy relating to the north-west. This means that you are a dignified, respectable and organised individual. You find it easy to command respect and others see you as a natural leader. At times, however, you prefer to opt out of conversation, instead sitting back and observing others.

7 6 6

dragon or ox

Your nine ki year number is to the north-west of your chart, which means that you have an air of dignity, enabling you to command respect and trust. You are also creative, imaginative and keen to communicate ideas. Your nine ki year number is opposite the number five and this means that you will find life easier if you go with the flow and wait for things come to you.

The dragon increases the ki energy of south-east further, giving you an active imagination and a desire to see your ideas realised. You can be a little self-righteous at times, and are very offended when your dignity is hurt.

The ox to the north-east makes you motivated and conscientious. Organisation is one of your strengths and you devote a lot of time to your work, often at the expense of friends and family. You are intuitive and usually find that you do the right thing instinctively.

8 6 7

sheep

Your nine ki year number is situated in the west, increasing the ki energy associated with financial awareness, romance and pleasure. You are likely to be ambitious, active and dynamic.

The month ki energy of the sheep increases the aspects of the chart in the south-west. This means that you value friends, family and home life very highly. At times, though, you tend to drift through life before managing to pick up momentum in a new direction.

9 6 8

dog

The ki energy along the north-east, south-west axis of your chart is increased, making you motivated, competitive and direct. You are quick to spot exciting opportunities and are also gifted at developing very good long-term relationships with friends and family.

The dog increases ki energy relating to the north-west. This gives you great organisational abilities and leadership skills. You are highly intuitive, but sometimes you lack tenacity and give in too easily.

7 nine ki birth chart

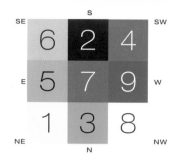

5 Number five is situated in the east so you have a powerful ability to gather a team of people together and inspire them to begin a new project. Your enthusiasm can be infectious and this quality endears you to others. However, because five ki energy changes, you can temporarily lose interest or direction. The combination of five and the east means you can become irritable with others and experience anger. If progress in achieving your considerable ambitions is blocked, you may feel frustrated and, eventually, resentful.

The soil ki energy of five is harmonious with the metal ki energy of seven at the centre of your chart, but is not harmonious with the tree ki energy of the east. This means that new projects may not work out as you hoped. However, once you find the right project, you have the ability to persevere and build up it quickly.

6 Moving clockwise to the south-east of your chart finds number six. This number is associated with being dignified, respected and in control, while the south-east relates to communication, creativity and imagination. This suggests that you can be creative, extremely imaginative and can communicate your ideas in an organised manner that is readily understood. However, as six is diagonally opposite its normal position in the magic square, others may not always take your meaning as you intend, which can create difficulties through lack of comprehension.

The metal ki energies of six and seven, the central number of your chart, make it easy for you to move into situations requiring communication. However, metal ki energy is not harmonious with the tree ki energy of the south-east, increasing the risk of misunderstandings in the long term.

2 Positioned at the south of your chart is the energy of number two. This number is associated with being cautious, careful and practical whereas the southern direction is associated with emotions, reputation and self expression. The combination means that you tend to be careful about your image and try hard to cultivate your reputation. You also tend to find practical ways to promote yourself. It is easy for you to project your more caring side and build up a social life, establishing long-term friendships along the way.

The soil ki energy associated with number two is harmonious with the fire ki energy related to the south, and is also harmonious with the metal ki energy of seven, the number found at the centre of your chart. This means you are a sociable individual and you find it easy to get noticed and express yourself.

4 Four occupies the south-western position of your chart. This direction is associated with friendships, family and the home, whereas four is associated with being persistent, creative and imaginative. This means you have a natural interest in homes, food, people, the environment and social issues, and you may find that these aspects of your life become increasingly important to you. As the south-west relates to the mother you would generally have a harmonious relationship with your mother and could enjoy a happy family life.

The soil ki energy relating to number two is harmonious with the metal ki energy of number seven at the centre of your chart, but it is not harmonious with the tree ki energy of four. This means that you find it easy to move into these aspects of your life, but can risk frustration and disappointment in the long term.

9 The western position of your chart is occupied by the number nine. The west is associated with romance, financial income and pleasure, while nine relates to being passionate, emotional and social. This means that you are often fervent about your romantic relationships and also have an emotional attachment to accumulating money and material wealth. You can generate a lot of energy in these areas of your life when you are feeling emotionally well and enjoy the people involved with you. At other times, however, you may feel a distinct lack of enthusiasm for such endeavours. As the number nine is opposite the powerful ki energy of five, there is a greater risk that you can feel blocked in terms of romance or financial income and that the pursuit of pleasure can create problems.

The fire ki energy of number nine is not in harmony with the metal ki energies of the west or of seven, the number at the centre of your chart. This increases the risk that these aspects of your life will not run smoothly.

8 The ki energy of the number eight occupies the north-western position of your birth chart. This direction is associated with leadership, organisation and dignity, while the number eight is associated with being motivated, competitive and quick. This means that you are quick to seize opportunities in leadership roles and are happy to take on greater responsibility. You tend to work hard in a leadership role and are a natural motivator of people. Other people can find you inspiring and stimulating. Although you are also well organised, you may find that you try to control other people too much, which can cause resentment.

The soil ki energy of eight is harmonious with the metal ki energies of the north-west and seven, the number at the centre of your chart. This makes it easier for you to assume responsibility and push forwards into leadership positions. It also means that you feel comfortable in these roles and can effortlessly maintain them in the long term.

3 Number three occupies the northern position of your chart. This direction is associated with spirituality, sex and independence, while three relates to being ambitious, active and dynamic. This means you tend to be analytical about spirituality and you need to understand how it works before you can abandon yourself and embrace it. Sexually you can be energetic and enjoy an active sex life. You find sex a positive force in your life and, at times, use it to give yourself a boost.

The tree ki energy of three is not harmonious with the metal ki energy of seven at the centre of your birth chart, but is harmonious with the water ki energy of the north. This means that sex with a new person may not be satisfying initially, but once established, should become a source of great satisfaction.

1 The energy of number one occupies the north-eastern direction of your birth chart. This is a direction that is associated with motivation, hard work and seizing new opportunities, whereas the number one is associated with being independent, objective and flexible. This means that you are flexible in the way you work and, when the situation presents itself, you can go with the flow. You can work very hard when you want to, but, equally, you enjoy times of rest and can even seem lazy.

The water ki energy of number one is harmonious with the metal ki energy of seven, the number at the centre of your chart, but not with the soil ki energy of the north-east. This means you can seize opportunities to move into hard-working and competitive situations, but find these roles hard to sustain.

1 7 8

rabbit or rat

Your nine ki year number is to the north-east of your chart, increasing the ki energy along this axis. This makes you competitive, self-motivated and hard working. You are clever in business, blending your natural charm with shrewd judgement. You also enjoy a secure family life and close friendships.

The month ki energy of the rabbit increases the energy of the east. This gives you the desire to go out and make things happen. You are ambitious and career orientated, but you may have less ki energy actually to complete tasks and keep a focus on the end result. You can become distracted with new ideas.

The month ki energy of the rat produces greater ki energy relating to the north. This gives you objectivity, independence and sexuality but decreases your passion, expressiveness and sociability. You sometimes need to retreat into your own space without interference and may find comfort in spirituality in times of difficulty.

2 7 9

horse

Your nine ki year number is to the south, increasing the flow of energy along this axis. You are independent but sociable and you love to be noticed. You are also generous, expressive and enjoy sexuality.

The ki energy of the horse further increases the fiery ki energy of south. This enhances your popularity and expressiveness. You are an emotional individual and are very passionate about your feelings. You can at times be rather

hot-headed. You also have a tendency to worry unnecessarily about things. There is a chance that you occasionally feel uncomfortable in your own company, preferring to spend time with friends.

3 7 1

rooster

Your nine ki year number is to the north, increasing the ki energy along this axis in your chart. The result is that you are independent and spiritual, but also sociable and sexual. You love using your charm to find a sexual partner. You can switch from being warm and expressive to being rather clinical about life.

The rooster increases the aspects of the chart in the west relating to romance, pleasure and money matters. You are slightly cautious about starting new projects, but this reserve may be offset by your year number.

4 7 2

rabbit or rat

Your year number is to the south-west which increases the ki energy along this axis. This strengthens the aspect of your chart relating to forming friendships, refining skills and being practical. You are also motivated, competitive, quick-witted and great at working in a team. You have a clear sense of what you want to do in life, but you are also inclined to be cautious and careful.

The rabbit increases the ki energy in the east. As this is also the location of the powerful ki energy of five it gives this part of your chart greater influence. You tend to rush into new projects with enthusiasm and ambition, but there is a risk that your high expectations will not be realised.

The rat increases ki energy relating to the north. This gives you objectivity, independence and sexuality. You can look at situations clearly and dispassionately, but may be inclined to be less sociable, expressive or even truly passionate.

5 7 3

horse

Your nine ki year number is to the east of your chart, activating this axis. You start new projects with power and enthusiasm, but you can find it hard to control your temper if things do not go your way. You are ambitious in terms of wealth and also in your relationships.

The horse increases the fiery ki energy of the south. This increases your ability to be sociable and stand out in a crowd. You are passionate about things and people, but you can find it hard to be independent and objective. You may take time to recover from ill health.

6 7 4

rooster

Your nine ki year number is to the south/east, making you an effective communicator and great at expressing your ideas. You can explain things in a logical, well reasoned manner. You are also persistent, organised and excellent in a leadership position.

The rooster increases the aspects of the chart in the west that relate to romance, pleasure and money – areas in which you have strength and passion. However, you are cautious about new beginnings and any dramatic changes.

7 7 5

rabbit or rat

Your nine ki year number is in the centre of your chart, strengthening all the aspects of your emotional characteristics defined by your month number on page 31. You use your charm to win people over – they find you great fun. You

pursue ambitions and gain material wealth, but may go through times of deep depression.

The rabbit increases the ki energy of the east. Your ambition and desire to take on new challenges are heightened. You can be too ambitious, however, and failure to attain your goals can result in frustration and temper.

The rat means greater ki energy relating to the north. This makes you more objective, independent and sexual. You are good at charming the opposite sex, but you can lack true passion and self-expression.

8 7 6

horse

Your nine ki year number is to the north-west of your chart. You are organised and conduct yourself with dignity, making it easy for people to trust you. You naturally gravitate towards positions of leadership or responsibility and communicate ideas with authority.

The horse increases the fiery ki energy of the south. You are expressive and love being at the centre of social occasions. You are also emotional and passionate but find it hard to be independent and objective. Health problems may be difficult to shake off. You may choose to spend time with friends rather than on your own.

9 7 7

rooster

You have increased energy along the west to east axis of your chart. This axis also has the ki energy of five. Romance, completing projects and finance are highlighted. You are also ambitious and focussed but, at times, these areas of your life feel blocked.

The rooster further augments the aspects of the chart in the west. Romance, pleasure and financial awareness are of importance to you, but you can be apprehensive about making changes and starting new projects. All this will need to be balanced with other aspects of your life.

nine ki birth chart

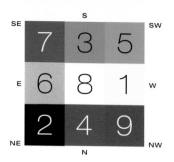

5 Number five is situated in the south-west position of your chart. This means you have a powerful ability to make an impression and can form deep relationships with friends and family. As the ki energy of five changes, there is an increased risk of confrontations and you may find it harder to maintain these relationships in the long-term. The south-west relates to the mother so your relationship with her may consist of great extremes, even more so if you are female.

The south-west and five both have soil ki energies and this is harmonious with the soil ki energy of eight, the number at the centre of your chart. This makes it easier for you to participate in family life. This aspect is made more powerful because the north-east, centre and south-west are all occupied by soil ki energy numbers, making it easy for ki energy to flow along this diagonal axis.

1 Moving clockwise to the west of your chart is one. This number relates to being independent, sexual and objective, whereas the west is associated with romance, financial awareness and finishing projects. You therefore tend to have an objective view of romantic relationships, but consider sex to be an important aspect. In fact, your independent streak can be clouded by your strong sexual desires. Your route to wealth may change many times, but once you find a way of making money you are successful. However, your ability to spend money can make it harder to save.

The water ki energy of one is not harmonious with the soil ki energy of eight, your central number, but it is harmonious with the metal ki energy of the west. This means it is hard for you to begin romantic relationships and find ways of making money, but once started it becomes easier.

9 To the north-west of your chart is nine. This number is associated with being passionate, fiery and expressive, whereas the north-west is related to leadership, organisation and dignity. You are often proud and will passionately defend your dignity, finding it hard to admit or accept your mistakes. You can put a lot of emotional energy into reaching a position of authority and responsibility and, as a leader, you are able to inspire people with your passionate beliefs. You are also able to develop warm relationships with others through your generous and affectionate nature.

The north-west is associated with the father, so you probably enjoy a close relationship with your father, although you may argue and lose closeness later on in life. If you are female, you tend to look for a romantic partner who is warm-hearted and capable of expressing his emotions.

4 The ki energy of number four occupies the northern position of your birth chart. This direction is associated with sex, spirituality and healing, whereas the number four is associated with being creative, imaginative and persistent. You therefore tend to be imaginative and have interesting ideas on spirituality. In fact, spirituality becomes an increasingly important part of your life as you get older. You also have the ability to heal yourself and can focus this ki energy to help heal others. You are usually comfortable with sex and enjoy sexual activities.

The tree ki energy of four is harmonious with the water ki energy of the north, but it is not harmonious with the soil ki energy of eight at the centre of your chart. This means you may find it hard to develop your spiritual side at first, but once you do, this aspect of your ki energy takes off.

2 The north-eastern position of your chart is occupied by two. This number is associated with being practical, realistic and caring, whereas the north-east relates to motivation, hard work and competition. As a consequence you tend to be practical in terms of work and can pursue goals realistically by building positive relationships with colleagues. In competitive situations, however, you may become jealous. Two is opposite its normal position in the magic square, so you might think you are doing the things you need to win, but your efforts may be misdirected, allowing others to claim victory. Two is also opposite the powerful number five, so you may feel blocked when trying to find or develop a new direction in life.

As two, the north-east and eight (the number at the centre of your chart) are all soil ki energies, it is easier for you to seize an opportunity and build on it quickly. You can also move easily between being motivated and quick, and careful or cautious.

6 The ki energy of number six occupies the eastern position of your birth chart. This direction is associated with ambition, activity and starting projects, whereas the number six is associated with being dignified, organised and in control. This means that you will be effective at planning and organising a new project or business venture, and are able to set far-reaching goals and work steadily towards them. You will also find it easy to start a project with dignity. This helps you to win the respect and trust of others, making it easier for you to enlist their support. You take your career seriously and are disciplined and responsible in practice.

The metal ki energy of number six is harmonious with the soil ki energy of number eight at the centre of your chart, but it is not harmonious with the tree ki energy of the east. This means that you may find it easy to get started on a new venture, but the longer you keep working on it, the greater the risk of frustration setting in if progress is not made smoothly.

7 The south-eastern position of your chart is occupied by seven. This number relates to being stylish, romantic and playful, while the south-east is associated with communication, creativity and persistence. The combination allows you to communicate your ideas with style and panache, and appear charismatic and charming in front of an audience. You can also be highly entertaining and make people laugh.

The metal ki energy of seven is harmonious with the soil energy of the eight at the centre of your chart, but is not harmonious with the metal ki energy of the south-east. This means you are most effective when you need to make a big impression quickly, but there is a risk that your charm can wear thin if you become overexposed to an audience or spend too much time making your point.

3 Three occupies the southern position of your chart. This direction is associated with public recognition, self expression and pride, while three is associated with being ambitious, active and enthusiastic. You therefore tend to be an active self-publicist and are enthusiastic when given the opportunity to express yourself, shining in public situations. However, you can rush into these situations without a clear plan.

The tree ki energy of three is harmonious with the fire ki energy of the south, but not with the soil ki energy of eight at the centre. This means you can misrepresent yourself, and others may find you pretentious and superficial. However, once you relax and get to know a person, you will be seen as genuinely positive and inspirational and will be able to develop deep, close relationships.

1 8 7

tiger or boar

Your nine ki year number is situated to the west, activating the flow of ki energy along this axis of your chart. You are romantic, playful and enjoy pleasures in life. You are also ambitious, active and are good at focussing on the end result of a project. You can spot chances to make a profit.

The month ki energy of the tiger increases the north-eastern ki energy. This gives you motivation and a desire to compete. You have a good business sense and are able to make quick decisions. You also have a reckless streak and you can be accused of neglecting family and friends.

The boar means greater ki energy relating to the north-west. This gives you dignity, organisational abilities and leadership potential. It is easy for you to gain trust and respect. Sometimes, however, you can be rather uncommunicative, preferring to sit back and observe people.

2 8 8

snake

Your nine ki year number is situated in the north-east, increasing the ki energy associated with being competitive, quick and motivated. You have a fighting spirit and like to take on new challenges. However, as your nine ki year number is opposite the number five, you could feel that these strengths are sometimes blocked. You also value family and friends and create a warm home.

The snake increases the ki energy of the south-east. You love using your imagination and communicating your ideas. You are effective at public speaking, but you find it difficult to plan ahead. You can be insecure if you feel that things are not within your control.

3 8 9

monkey

You have an increase of ki energy along the south to north axis of your chart. This is the ki energy associated with social life, self expression and emotion. You have an excellent ability to promote yourself, be noticed and are independent, objective and sexual.

The month ki energy of the monkey strengthens the aspects of the chart in the south-west, relating to family, friendships and the home. You may go through periods when you lack motivation and lose direction.

4 8 1

tiger or boar

Your nine ki year number is to the north of your chart, increasing the ki energy along this axis. You tend to be independent, sexual and objective. Material wealth is very important to you and you are shrewd when it comes to business. You are also sociable, expressive and find it easy to promote yourself. You can move effortlessly and comfortably from one situation to the next.

The tiger means an increase in the ki energy of the north-east. This chart also combines the ki energy of the year number five and the animal along one axis making this ki energy exceptionally strong and hard to control. You like to be motivated, compete and work hard, although work may not go smoothly. Any upsets in this area of your life can have a major impact, making it hard to settle down again.

The month ki energy of the boar gives greater ki energy relating to the north-west. This gives you organisational abilities and leadership potential. You also have a great deal of dignity. You present yourself as someone to be trusted and you command great respect from others. However, you may not find it easy to be creative, expressive and imaginative.

5 8 2
snake

Your nine ki year number is to the south-west. You form good relationships with friends, family and clients, but as your year number five is in this location, your rash changes may jeopardise these relationships. You also work hard, but risk going to extremes.

The snake increases the ki energy of south-east. You are imaginative, expressive and tenacious. You can be disorganised, though, and struggle to manage your time.

6 8 3
monkey

Your nine ki year number is to the east, increasing the ki energy along this axis in your chart. The result is that you tend to be not only ambitious but also enthusiastic about implementing your ideas. You can visualise and focus on the completion of a project.

The month ki energy of the monkey increases the aspects of the chart in the south-west that relate to relationships with friends, family and colleagues. You form successful long-term relationships and value the people you are close to. You may at times lack motivation and you could become apathetic towards work.

7 8 4
tiger or boar

Your nine ki year number is to the south-east, relating to communication, creativity and persistence, whilst also activating the energy associated with organisation and responsibility. You are an effective, clear communicator, if

you have time to plan ahead. You also have an air of dignity and are able to command respect.

The month ki energy of the tiger increases the ki energy of the north-east. As this is combined with the number five, there is greater strength along this axis. You have a desire to compete, work hard and win. You may lack energy to devote to loved ones, though.

The boar provides ki energy relating to the north-west. This is the same axis as your year number, increasing the ki energy. You are organised and possess leadership skills. You take on responsibilities with ease, but may have less ki energy for persistence.

8 8 5
snake

Your nine ki year number is in the centre of your chart, strengthening the aspects of your characteristics as defined by your month number on page 51. You are focussed, and enjoy competition and success.

The snake increases the ki energy of south-east. You are imaginative and need to communicate your ideas. You could find it difficult to win people's trust and sometimes feel that your dignity is compromised.

9 8 6
monkey

Your nine ki year number is to the north-west, which increases the ki energy along this axis. You have great dignity, love control and may easily become a leader. Your way of communicating ideas commands respect.

The month ki energy of the monkey increases the aspects of the chart in the south-west relating to friendships, family and home. These are of great value to you. You could go through periods when you lose momentum and find yourself drifting through life.

nine ki birth chart

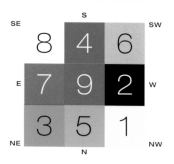

5 Number five is situated in the north of your chart, a direction that is related to sex, regeneration, healing and spirituality. This means that you have a powerful sexuality that draws people to you. You may also have strong healing or spiritual powers but find these hard to turn on at will. Because five ki energy is changeable, you may feel that you lose these powers at times, and go through periods of very little sexual activity. You can use this ki energy to recover from personal health problems, but again, you may experience periods of poor health from which you find it hard to recuperate.

The soil ki energy of five is harmonious with the fire ki energy of nine at the centre of your chart, but not with the water ki energy of the north. This means that it is easy for you to move into sexual, healing or spiritual activities, but you may find it hard to keep up these levels of passion.

3 Moving clockwise to the north-east position of your chart is the ki energy of number three. This number is associated with being aggressive, active and ambitious, while the north-east direction is associated with hard work, motivation and competitiveness. You therefore tend to be ambitious, but can only achieve your goals through hard work. One way to motivate yourself is to make loud, ambitious claims that put you in direct competition with someone else.

The tree ki energy of number three is harmonious with the fire ki energy of nine, the number at the centre of your chart, but it is not harmonious with the soil ki energy of the north-east. This means that you find it relatively easy to move quickly into a competitive, hard-working situation, but find it harder to pace yourself in such a way that you can last the course.

7 To the eastern position of your birth chart is the nine ki energy of number seven. This number is associated with pleasure, romance and contentment while the eastern direction is associated with activity, ambition and putting ideas into action. This combination means that you are able to realise your ambitions in life by being charming. You bring a sense of fun and pleasure into your work and this is usually one of your best strategies for succeeding.

As seven is opposite its normal position and the metal ki energy of seven is not harmonious with either the fire ki energy of nine (the number at the centre of your chart) or the tree ki energy of the east, your ambitions and ideas may not prove to be as realistic or attainable as you anticipated. When faced with difficulties, you are tempted to give up and try something else.

8 The number eight occupies the south-east position of your chart. This direction is associated with communication, creativity and imagination, while eight is associated with being direct, sharp and piercing. As a result, you communicate in a particularly persuasive manner, and when you are annoyed you can be unpleasantly sharp and direct. When critical, your voice and choice of words are cold and have a biting edge. In terms of creativity, your imagination can have great clarity and you can be particularly insightful.

The soil ki energy of number eight is harmonious with the fire ki energy of nine, the number at the centre of your chart, but it is not harmonious with the tree ki energy of the south-east. This means that you can rush into speaking your mind, only to find that this causes difficulties in the long run.

4 The southern position of your birth chart is occupied by the nine ki energy of number four. This number is associated being imaginative, creative and persistent, and also with travel and distribution. The southern direction is associated with passion, self expression and public recognition. This means that your ability to become excited about something is infectious and you are able to communicate this passion to others, making you an exciting person to be around. As the ki energy of number four also represents your destiny, you can look to this area of your chart for long-term success in being noticed, becoming famous or developing lots of social connections. You may also develop a passion for travel.

The tree ki energy of nine ki number four is harmonious with the fire ki energy of the south and the fire ki energy of number nine at the centre of your birth chart. This means that you are comfortable expressing your feelings and emotions to others.

6 Number six occupies the south-western position of your chart. This direction is associated with home, family, and food, while six relates to organisation, planning ahead and being in control. You therefore need to feel in control of your diet, family and living space, and find it hard to share authority or responsibility. You are usually highly organised in these areas of your life and take these responsibilities seriously. As the south-west relates to the mother, you may have had conflicts with your mother when you were growing up and were possibly quite a difficult child. However, this is tempered by a deep respect for your mother – indeed, you may have adopted many of her traits.

The metal ki energy of six is harmonious with the soil ki energy of the south-west, but not with the fire ki energy of nine at the centre of your chart. This means that you do not feel comfortable rushing into intimate relationships, preferring to build them up slowly over a period of time.

2 Two occupies the western position. This direction is associated with romance, financial awareness and pleasures, while two relates to being cautious, careful and dependent. In consequence you tend to be cautious when beginning a serious relationship, but once you overcome this initial reserve, you can form deep and long-lasting relationships. You find it hard to achieve independent financial success, feeling the need to align yourself with someone who has a more active energy in the west.

The soil ki energy of two is harmonious with the metal ki energy of the west but not with the fire energy of nine at the centre. This means that you may be disappointed if you rush into a money-making project or romance, but once you find the right venture or person, you are more likely to succeed.

1 One occupies the north-western direction in your chart. This direction is associated with organisation, planning ahead and leadership, while one is a deep, intuitive and spiritual ki energy. This means you have a laid back approach to leadership and are happy to let others take this role at work. You don't like planning ahead, except in home life, and prefer to rely on your good intuition. As the north-west relates to the father you may have an affectionate relationship with your father, but could become distant in later years.

The water ki energy of one is harmonious with the metal ki energy of the north-west, but not with the fire ki energy of nine at the centre. This means you can cause difficulties if you rush into leadership roles, but may be more successful in these positions if you are patient.

1 9 6

dog

Your nine ki year number is situated to the north-west of your chart which increases the presence of ki energy along this axis. You are good at organising and you like to feel in control. You can be self-righteous and will go to great lengths to prove that you are in the right and preserve your precious dignity.

The month ki energy of the dog leads to even greater ki energy relating to the north-west. This gives you even stronger organisational abilities, leadership potential and dignity. You are self-disciplined and like to plan ahead carefully. You may go through periods, however, when your creativity and imagination feel blocked.

2 9 7

dragon or ox

Ki energy along the axis running from west to east is strong, as your year number is situated in the west. You are financially aware, romantic and enjoy pleasures. You are particularly successful when working with others to increase your wealth. You are ambitious, and have a positive and enthusiastic attitude.

The ki energy of the dragon increases the ki energy of the south-east. This gives you creativity, inspiration and the desire to spread your ideas. You are enthusiastic about starting new projects, but you could find it hard to organise yourself and be punctual.

The ox is to the north-east and strengthens this ki energy in the chart, increasing motivation and competitive spirit. You have a direct approach and make quick

changes in your life when the opportunities arise. You may find that you have less ki energy for your friends and family, and you must ensure that you do not take advantage of these people.

3 9 8

sheep

You have an increase of ki energy along the north-east, south-west axis of your chart. This enhances the ki energy associated with competition and hard work. You are clear thinking, can spot opportunities and take them quickly. You also have great energy for developing long-term friendships and family relationships.

The month ki energy of the sheep further increases the aspects of the chart in the south-west that relate to family and friends, but being opposite your nine ki year number can make these areas hard to control. You could go through periods when you lose your normally powerful sense of direction.

4 9 9

dog

Your nine ki year number is to the south of your chart. The result is that you are sociable and find it easy to express yourself. You also have a strong independent streak. As your year number is opposite five, however, you can sometimes feel that your path is blocked.

The dog gives you more ki energy relating to the north-west. You have great integrity, respectability and good organisational skills. Sometimes you like to observe rather than participate in conversation.

5 9 1

dragon or ox

Your nine ki year number is to the north, increasing the flow of energy along this axis. You are independent and original in your ideas and lifestyle. You look at situations objectively and have strong sexuality, as well as a sense of spirituality. You enjoy the warmth of other people's company.

The dragon increases the ki energy of the south-east. You are artistic and enjoy sharing your ideas. You can be disorganised, however, particularly when it comes to time-keeping. You guard your dignity closely.

The ox to the north-east increases this ki energy. You are motivated and would excel in trade or any activity that involves speculation. You tend to make dramatic changes to your life when you feel stuck in a rut.

6 9 2

sheep

Your nine ki year number is to the south-west, increasing the ki energy along this axis. You are cautious, realistic and practical. You find it easier to do things as a part of a team rather than alone. You have great energy for long-term friendships and strong family relationships.

The month ki energy of the sheep further increases the aspects of the chart in the south-west that relate to friendships, family and home. Security and warmth are important to you. Sometimes you lack the motivation and competitive spirit to achieve things for yourself.

7 9 3

dog

Your nine ki year number is to the east, which increases the ki energy along this axis. It strengthens the aspect of your chart relating to ambition and activity. You implement ideas and bring them to a successful conclusion. You are also romantic and usually feel content.

The dog provides greater ki energy relating to the north-west. This gives you organisational abilities and leadership skills. You approach situations with wisdom, but have less ki energy for persistence and tenacity.

8 9 4

dragon or ox

Your nine ki year number is to the south-east of your chart, encouraging you to use your imagination, creativity and to generate new ideas. You are great at organising your ideas and are able to take on important responsibilities. You can be impatient to move things forward, however, since you like to see rapid progress.

The dragon increases the ki energy of the south-east even further. You are extremely imaginative and enjoy communicating your ideas. Your mind is so active that you can find it difficult to switch off. Sometimes, you feel that you lose control of situations and are a victim of circumstance.

The ox is to the north-east, increasing that ki energy. You are motivated and hard working, but this could be at the expense of spending time with friends and family. You find business opportunities particularly exciting and love to see a project taking shape.

9 9 5

sheep

Your nine ki year number is in the centre of your chart, strengthening the aspects of your emotional characteristics as defined by their month number on page 33. You have powerful emotions that you are able to channel into self-expression. You add feeling and warmth to whatever you do. You can easily gain the attention of others, which may make you self-centred.

The sheep increases the aspects of the chart in the south-west relating to friendships, family and colleagues. You have a natural ability to form good long-term relationships with people. You can be indecisive at times and go through periods of feeling insecure.

The nine different energies

As we have seen in the previous chapters, every feng shui number and direction is associated with a certain kind of energy. These nine different energies are also related to a specific season, time and month, as well as a trigram (see right), colour and member of a traditional Oriental family. These combine to give each energy a distinct character.

what are energies?

Each of the nine numbers in feng shui astrology has a certain character or 'energy'. The following pages help you to build up an appreciation of each type of energy by likening it to a different feature of nature, such as earth, thunder, wind, heaven, lake and mountain. This is most helpful if you have experienced the atmosphere they relate to, for example, being out in a thunderstorm or strong wind, climbing a mountain, working with the earth or sitting by a lake. However, you will need to use your imagination for heaven! Each ki energy is associated with an element (water, tree, fire, soil and metal), a direction, a time of day, a season, a trigram (see opposite) and a family member in a traditional Oriental household. It is important to familiarise yourself with the attributes of each energy or number as this knowledge will help you to interpret your birth chart (see pages 34–73).

Directions, times and seasons
The directions are best understood by thinking of the sun's position in the sky, and are linked to the times of day. This is largely governed by

the movement of the sun through the sky. The east relates to the sun rising, the south to the sun at its highest point in the sky, the west to the sunset and the north to darkness. The north-east, south-east, south-west and north-west each represent the change from one state to another.

By experiencing the atmosphere of each season, you can also gain an insight into the kind of ki energy that makes up a person's character. A person with a winter ki energy, for example, will be very different to a person with a summer ki energy. The months refer to the period in each year when each type of ki energy is at its highest. For example, during December water ki energy will be strongest. Check on page 20 to see when the nine ki months begin and end.

Colours

Each number or type of energy also has an associated colour. By surrounding yourself with that colour, you will help strengthen and reinforce the ki energy related to it. This is because coloured surfaces reflect light of different wavelengths and frequencies, so if you walked into a room where the floor, walls and ceiling were all painted red, your own ki energy would be influenced by the ki of all the reflected light waves – in this case the ki energy would make you feel more yang, aggressive, active and alert. If you walked from this room into one painted exclusively in pale blue, you would begin to feel more yin, calm, passive and relaxed.

To use these colours to your advantage, look at the trigrams on the right and find the colours that correspond to each number (five does not have a trigram but it is associated with the colour yellow). Each colour strengthens the qualities of that particular number, whether it be your year, month or axis number.

The attributes of each number

On the following pages you will find a complete description of each of the numbers or energies. The column on the left of these pages gives a summary of all the qualities associated with each of the nine ki energies. The last entry in the column on the right, Timing, tells you what you are likely to experience if your year number is in the direction associated with that number. This is because each year, your year number is immersed in a different type of energy, making it easier to achieve certain things in life while other ventures become more risky. In each of these phases people with particular year numbers will find life in general more comfortable (see also pages 107–17).

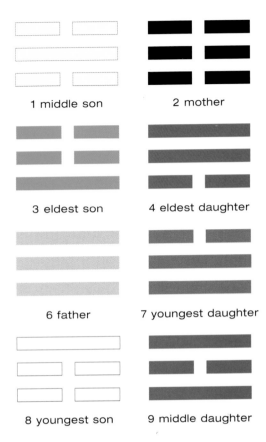

1 middle son

2 mother

3 eldest son

4 eldest daughter

6 father

7 youngest daughter

8 youngest son

9 middle daughter

The eight trigrams

A trigram is made up of three lines that are either broken or unbroken. An unbroken line represents yang and a broken line represents yin. Each trigram represents a member of a traditional Oriental family and the characteristics that they would typically have. For example, the father has three yang lines, which represents his dominance in the household. Note that the number five does not have a trigram.

1

water

north

night

(23.00–01.00)

winter

december

middle son

The number one is associated with water ki energy and also represents the night in the middle of winter. To experience this type of ki energy, you would need to go out in the middle of the night to a quiet location in the middle of winter. Ideally, it would be a dark, starry, moonlit night and you would be surrounded by water with either frost or snow on the ground. As you stood in these surroundings, you would become aware of the stillness around you. Your breathing and heartbeat would become more noticeable, and you would generally be more aware of yourself. In these circumstances it would be easier to gain access to some of your deepest spiritual feelings and beliefs. You would also find it easier to think objectively about your life and consider your circumstances in a more clinical and less emotional manner. This is what gives this type of ki energy a certain quality of independence.

The ability to reach inside and find your deepest feelings enables people who have one as their month number to be very affectionate and loving. However, such people also need their own space and at times can seem distant, aloof and disinterested as they retreat into deeper levels of this ki energy. When faced with difficulties, there is a tendency for people

Seeking shores

A person with the number one in his or her code needs containment. Without this, water individuals can become chaotic and undisciplined.

Lively and fresh

A spirit of adventure characterises people who have the number one in their code. This is a reflection of water's natural tendency to move on and over obstacles.

PERSONAL QUALITIES

Affectionate
Loving
Independent
Objective
Secretive
Flexible
Sexual
Spiritual

POSSIBLE CAREERS

Healer
Therapist
Member of a spiritual or religious order
Consultant or advisor
Musician
Artist
Gynaecologist
Sex-industry worker
Pharmacist

TIMING

Spiritual awareness and inner peace
Greater independence
An objective overview
Regeneration
Conception
More adventurous sex
The healing of old wounds
Intimacy and affection
Financial or health problems

Particularly favourable for those with year numbers 1, 3, 4 and 7.
6 needs to stay out of the public eye and guard against sexual scandals.

with this nine ki year number to run away or withdraw until they have worked things out. This ki energy is therefore ideal for keeping secrets or hiding away from danger.

The night time atmosphere associated with number one is conducive to being more spiritually orientated so this nine ki number is therefore associated with religion, spirituality and meditation. Winter is also a time when the soil regenerates itself for the following spring, just as night is a time for sleep in preparation for the next day's activities. As a year number, one is therefore associated with deep healing and personal regeneration, as well as conception and sex.

Water is the element that relates to number one. The fluid nature of water means it is an energy that can find its way through most obstacles. With sufficient momentum this energy also can be powerful and forceful, although it is found deep inside and is not apparent on the surface. Not surprisingly, many explorers have this number in their charts. People who have one as their month number are often extremely fluid speakers who can communicate their feelings well.

One represents the middle son, someone traditionally seen as becoming independent and leaving home comparatively early. The accompanying trigram has a yang line in the middle and yin lines above and below. This depicts inner strength surrounded by a more flexible, quiet force.

2

earth

soil

south-west

afternoon
(13.00–17.00)

summer to autumn

july & august

mother

The number two is associated with earth ki energy and also represents the afternoon and late summer. To feel this ki energy, you would need to go out during the afternoon to a quiet location at a time when summer is changing into autumn. Ideally, you would be surrounded by flat land and vegetation. As you stood in this environment, you would become aware of the surrounding vegetation starting to turn from green to brown and yellow. You would also start to notice the sun descending in the sky. The overriding impression would be of nature settling down. This is a time when, rather than continuing to grow, fruits, vegetables and grains ripen. The key to harnessing this energy is to make more of what you already have, rather than trying to expand further.

In such an atmosphere and ki energy it is easy to consolidate and improve the situation you already find yourself in. This ki energy can help you to be practical and carefully move forwards one step at a time. People who have the nine ki number two in their code tend to have a more realistic outlook on life. Two is also a useful energy for deepening and strengthening relationships, particularly friendships. At the same time, it is an energy that can lead to strong feelings of jealousy, indecision and insecurity. This is because there is no strong forwards direction.

The afternoon is the time relating to number two. Similar to the second half of something, this energy makes it easier for people to make improvements later on in their lives. Someone who has two as his or her

Enjoy the scenery
The number two
represents the change
from summer to
autumn, a time for
settling down and
making the most of
your achievements.

nine ki year number will often be careful and cautious, preferring to make slow, steady progress rather than a speedy one. The risk is that he or she may feel stuck in a rut and lack

Primal instinct

If you have the number two in your nine ki code of numbers, you will most likely have a motherly, nurturing and caring nature.

the inspiration required to start up new projects. This can lead to a feeling of dependence on others for inspiration, excitement and sparkle. At the same time, a person with number two in his or her code is often drawn to people who can offer security.

The direction relating to nine ki number two is south-west. The season associated to this ki energy relates to a time when plants become ripe and are ready for harvesting. This aspect of the energy allows people with this number to add quality to whatever it is they do. This makes them naturally adept at developing skills and they can become talented in the field of arts, crafts or music. They also find it easy to research and refine matters.

The element related to nine ki number two is soil, which is essentially nurturing. The idea is that soil provides the basic nutrients to support life. People with two as their nine ki month energy often have strong, caring natures and are good at looking after others. In general, they tend to be considerate and sympathetic. This also enables them to do well in all activities related to food, the home and the family .

The nine ki number two represents the mother, someone who is traditionally seen as kind, caring and good at taking care of others. The trigram is made up of three yin lines, which make the ki energy related to the number two essentially receptive, passive and yielding.

3

thunder

tree

east

dawn
(05.00–07.00)

spring

march

eldest son

The number three is associated with thunder ki energy and also represents the dawn and spring. To feel this ki energy, you would have to go out at sunrise to a quiet location in the springtime. Ideally, you would be surrounded by trees and tall grasses. As you stood still, you would be aware of the presence of fresh young spring buds, dew rising from the grass, and everything in nature generally waking up around you. The overriding impression is of a new beginning and rising ki energy. In this environment, it would be easier to feel that another day is in front of you, presenting new opportunities for you to embrace. The atmosphere is conducive to being positive, ambitious and confident. The newness of this energy encourages you to be active, generate ideas and focus your mind on particular thoughts.

The number three is also a helpful ki energy for concentrating on details. In the right environment, you not only can generate new, ambitious ideas, but you also can actively set about putting them into action. It is generally a forward-thinking energy that is focussed on the future.

As this ki energy relates to the beginning of something, it is easy for someone with this nine ki year energy to make a quick start and achieve success early on in his or her life. There is a tendency to keep starting new projects, and this can lead to a situation where something is not worked through to a profitable conclusion before another is started. Someone with this nine ki year or month energy may tend to be too focussed and overlook the big picture, which can lead to missed opportunities. There is also a tendency to dismiss people or possibilities too quickly.

East is the direction that relates to number three. Just as with spring, eastern energy relates to a time associated with a plant sprouting its shoot and

New beginnings

Three energy is active, focussed and, similar to young shoots, represents a time of ambition, potential and upward growth.

Thunderous nature

A person with three in his or her code often can be quick to react, intolerant and verbally aggressive, especially when frustrated. But, like a thunderstorm, this mood is usually momentary.

taking in nutrients from the sun and air. It is a phase in which the plant grows rapidly, and people with this nine ki year energy are often able to generate growth and expansion in a business. The new shoots and buds are associated with new life and therefore this ki energy can also pertain to letting go of the past and moving on.

Tree is the element that relates to number three ki energy. The growth of the tree and the movement of sap up the trunk gives this ki energy a strong, upward thrusting movement. Thunder, the energy associated with the number three, adds the features of noise, quick reactions and the ability to make things happen rather than to passively wait for them to occur. A person whose code of numbers includes three is often impatient and can be prone to losing his or her temper easily, as well as shouting, particularly if this is the individual's nine ki month number. When especially frustrated, such a person can become aggressive. However, like a thunder storm, this is short lived and quickly forgotten.

Three represents the eldest son, who is traditionally regarded as ambitious, enthusiastic and keen to take over his father's responsibilities. The trigram for three has one yang line with two yin lines above it. This represents the active yang energy being able to suddenly rise through the yin energy and quickly subside again.

4

wind

tree

south-east

morning
(07.00–11.00)

late spring

april & may

eldest daughter

The number four is associated with wind ki energy and also represents the morning and late spring. To feel this ki energy, you would need to go out to a quiet location in the morning during late spring. Ideally, you would be surrounded by trees and tall grasses. As you stood still, you would be aware of the sun rising in the sky. As the temperature increased you would become aware of a rising energy indicating that this is a time of activity.

The time relating to number four is close to the beginning of the day and leads to the midday sun. Number four therefore has a ki energy that is conducive to getting things done and building up one's life – although compared to when the sun is in the east, this energy is not as powerful. The advantage of four ki energy is that it allows you to do things in a more harmonious way, compared to number three energy (whose direction is east). Any work done when your year number is in the number four or south-east position is most helpful in terms of future prosperity. Number four is therefore a ki energy that relates to your future destiny.

Similar to three, the element related to nine ki number four is the tree. As a tree can be mature while still actively growing, it is easier for someone who has four in his or her code to make consistent progress throughout his or her life. His or her mind is very imaginative and tends to generate new ideas quickly. For this reason, others can find it hard to keep up with such a person's train of thought. If the individual updates his or her plans very quickly with new ideas, others may find them hard to follow.

People who have four as their month number can also can get lost in their own day dreams and will often be able to do more than one thing at the same time. They may be able to read a book, watch television and think about what they need to do for the following day all at once. When talking to such people, it can be difficult to tell whether they are really concentrating on what you are saying or thinking about something else.

Persistent and tenacious

People with four in their code can find it hard to forget and let go, especially when they feel they have been maltreated.

Soft hues of spring
Compared to the springtime season that is also related to number three, four's springtime season is more uplifting, gentle and soft.

PERSONAL QUALITIES

Quick to generate new ideas
Desire to communicate ideas
Sensitive
Persistent
Imaginative
Creative
Harmony seeking

POSSIBLE CAREERS

Writer
Editor
Designer
Film director
Script writer
Actor
Media executive
Distributor
Travel consultant
Marketing consultant

TIMING

Generating new ideas that could lead to future prosperity
Getting engaged or married
Communicating your ideas successfully
Being creative
Travelling
Thinking on a global level
Expanding a business
Being too persistent
Not taking advice

Favourable for those with year numbers 1, 4 and 9. 3 may have trouble with relationships.

Wind is the energy associated with number four and this represents the spreading of ideas (wind blows seeds, allowing them to reproduce over a wide area). Someone who has four as his or her year or month number will often have a strong desire to communicate ideas, whether it be through talking, writing, art, film or music. This type of ki energy can also instill an enthusiasm to travel or be involved in things associated with travel, such as cars, trains and planes.

The ki energy of wind is more persistent than thunder, but not as loud. Therefore, someone with this ki energy can be very determined and tenacious, often cunningly getting his or her own way.

Four represents the eldest daughter, someone who is traditionally seen as being gentle, kind and sensitive. This can often lead to a situation where someone with this nine ki month energy takes negative remarks or criticism too personally. Generally, a person with this ki energy will tend to shy away from confrontation.

The trigram relating to number four has one yin line at the bottom and two yang lines above it. This combines the changeable nature of wind with power and speed. This characteristic can lead to people having mood swings combined with a forceful nature.

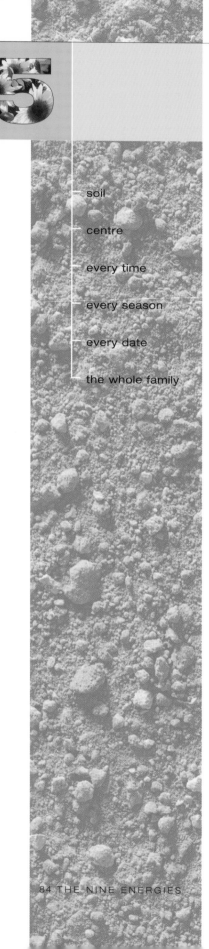

soil

centre

every time

every season

every date

the whole family

The ki energy of number five is the most powerful of all the nine types of energy. This is because it is at the centre of the magic square and is therefore at the centre of each axis of ki energy. All the other ki energies must pass through five to reach any of the others, so nine ki number five influences and controls all the other ki energies. On the other hand, nine ki number five is influenced by all the other eight types of ki energy. In this respect it is the most changeable and volatile type of ki energy and the combination of power and volatility means that the ki energy relating to five can be used to achieve great things. But, equally, it can be a self-destructive energy.

In terms of the time of day and season, the energy relating to nine ki number five represents all the times and every season. This can make it the hardest ki energy to imagine or sense. It is not only a case of anything can happen, but also that it happens with great force.

A person with five as his or her nine ki year or month number will frequently end up in the centre of activities and often likes to be the centre of attention. At the same time, these people commonly find themselves easily influenced by others. People with the number five in their code have the advantage of being able to understand people with all the other types of ki energy. They can change their minds easily depending on the opinions around them, and, at the same time, can bring great power to bear on something. In this sense they can be confrontational and argumentative and, as they can easily win, they make the 'losers' feel particularly uncomfortable.

People who have five as their year number often find they go through many changes in their lives. Usually their most successful strategy is to be as stable as possible and to be ready to make the most of opportunities as

Hearth of the matter
People with five in their code place an importance on family life and are home-oriented people.

they arise. This approach will work best when they are at the centre of things.

A person with number five in his or her code usually has a large circle of friends and, ideally, would have a job which involves being surrounded by lots of other people. If such an individual has been brought up with good social skills and has cultivated the ability to influence people, he or she can achieve many things.

At times, people with number five in their code can go through periods when nothing happens and they may feel that their lives are stagnating. The worst situation is if they are isolated, in which case they become starved of the ki energy they need to function. People with number five ki energy need to be careful not to be too confrontational or argumentative, or take friends for granted.

Soil is the element relating to nine ki number five. Soil adds an element of stability, although at times it can become a predominant force and someone with this energy can feel as though he or she is stuck in a rut and going through periods where nothing seems to be happening.

Because number five is a special number, there is no single trigram or specific family member that is associated with this ki energy.

A yellow powerhouse

The number five is the most powerful energy in nine ki astrology. Just like the seeds of a sunflower, nine ki number five is positioned at the centre of the magic square and its energy is concentrated there.

PERSONAL QUALITIES

Powerful
Can mix with all types of people
Thrives on attention
Attracts opportunities
Sympathetic
Potentially influential
Home-orientated

POSSIBLE CAREERS

Politician
Member of religious order
Mediator
Power broker
Farmer
Food-related industry worker
Builder
Architect
Construction worker

TIMING

Experiencing change
Attracting new opportunities
Understanding other people
Achieving greater power
Influencing others
Being influenced by others
Avoiding major changes
Taking things as they come

Favourable for those with year numbers 2, 5, 6, 7, 8 and 9.

heaven

metal

north-west

evening to night
(19.00–23.00)

autumn to winter

october & november

father

The number six is associated with heaven ki energy and also represents the evening changing to night at a time when autumn turns into winter. To feel this type of ki energy, you would need to go out after sunset to a quiet location as autumn is changing to winter. Ideally you would be surrounded by rolling hills and large rounded rocks. As you stood still you would be aware of everything moving inwards as nature prepares for night. In this environment, it would be easier to reflect on the events of the past, be it that day or that year, and consider how you might have improved things. This quality gives people with the number six as their nine ki year or month energy an ability to be wise. It is also a useful ki energy for planning ahead to the next year and being better organised.

Metal is the element related to the number six and it is a ki energy that is solid, responsible and reliable. People with the nine ki number six as their year or month number are capable of achieving high levels of self discipline and self control. They also value dignity and self respect and would be deeply hurt if they were made a fool of. They tend to seek the company of people they respect and show great loyalty to them. They are also honest, and although this is an admirable trait, they may offend others by making rather blunt, personal statements. The metal energy tends to make these people place a high value on material wealth. Financial security is often a particular priority and without it they can worry and feel tense. People with this number in their code may also use material wealth to gain prestige, dignity and respect.

North-west is the direction related to number six and this ki energy relates to a time when the harvested crops and vegetables are prepared so that they last over the winter. This enables people with number six in their code to take a long-term view on life and work methodically towards long-term goals. These people are fortunate in that they can often work through setbacks and keep going, even when they encounter difficulties. Their best strategy towards achieving success is often to take a slower, more methodical route than others on the path to success.

Solid as a rock

Six has the most yang energy of all the numbers, so people with six in their code are considered strong and stable.

PERSONAL QUALITIES

Honest

Intuitive

Perceptive

Organised

Responsible

Respectable

Loyal

Self disciplined

Dignified

Natural leader

POSSIBLE CAREERS

Politician

Manager

Healer

Teacher

Management consultant

Planner/organiser

Administrator

Engineer

Heaven is the symbol associated with number six and this gives people an ability to reach the earth's outer spheres of ki energy, providing a strong spiritual dimension to their characters. People who have number six in their code can therefore be perceptive and intuitive.

Bright lights, big city

The energy of number six is similar to the structured and organised lifestyle that people have when they live in big cities.

Number six represents the father, who is traditionally seen as a voice of authority and a natural leader who is keen to take responsibility for others. This can give people with the number six in their code a more self-righteous attitude in which they readily pass moral judgements on others. At times, the standard they expect from others are so high they cannot live up to it themselves, and this factor may make them seem rather hypocritical. If unchecked, they can appear negative, severe and critical to others, although this is not their intention. It is usually important for these people to feel in control of situations, so they are happiest in a leadership position or when they are working for themselves. They do not like being told what to do. In family situations there is a risk that people with number six ki energy can exert too much control over other members of the family, which can make them overbearing and dictatorial. This aspect can appear intimidating to others.

The trigram relating to number six consists of three yang lines. This reflects the most yang form of ki energy there is.

TIMING

A promotion

Self discipline

Intuition

Better organisation

Finding a mentor

Dignity

Being able to plan ahead

Becoming self-employed

Being more decisive

Being self-righteous and overbearing

Favourable for those with year numbers 1, 2, 5, 6 and 8.
7 may have trouble communicating.

7

lake

metal

west

sunset
(17.00–19.00)

autumn

september

youngest
daughter

The number seven represents lake ki energy and also the sunset during the autumn. To feel this ki energy, you would need to go out at sunset to a quiet location in the autumn. Ideally, you would be surrounded by round rolling hills and large stones. As you stood still, you would be aware of the landscape resolving into a point as the sun disappeared below the horizon at the end of the day. In this environment, it would be easier for you to focus on the end of a project. You would find it easier to think of ways to bring matters to a successful conclusion and make a project more profitable.

The energy associated with number seven can help you work consistently towards the end of your life. This ki energy is also conducive to being able to reassess projects you have undertaken and think how you would be able to do the same thing again with a better end result.

Sunset is the time of day related to nine ki number seven, and the end of a good day is a time to relax and feel content with your efforts. People who have seven in their code want to enjoy the pleasures of life. As the end of the day would be a favourable time to be more romantically orientated, these people also enjoy being in a romantic relationship and can be enthusiastic sexual partners. People with seven as their nine ki year number often need regular, pleasurable activities and tend to be motivated when uncomfortable. For example, if such individuals do not have enough money to indulge in their tastes, then they will find ways to earn more. However, once such people have achieved their goals, it is easy for them to become lazy and lose their motivation.

West is the direction related to seven ki energy and autumn is the season related to seven. This is a time associated with the harvest, in particular, reaping the rewards of all your hard work. It is similar to the traditional practice of being paid at the end of the working day.

For people who have seven as their nine ki year number it is important to be able to see the end result. As long as they can

Sunset scenario

A sunset will capture the romantic nature of seven. Round shapes and domes are also related to this energy.

Bright and shiny
An attraction to material goods often symbolises a person who has seven in his or her code.

see the light at the end of the tunnel and have something to look forwards to, these people will be able to work positively towards their goals. However, once they can no longer see the potential outcome of their efforts, they can easily lose motivation and give up.

Metal is the element related to number seven and this symbolises material possessions. A person who has seven in his or her code therefore has a tendency to be attracted to material things. Money is also often important to someone with the nine ki number seven. In addition, metal is associated with precious metals and jewellery, which often results in people with this nine ki number having a particular sense of style and appreciation of beauty.

The energy associated with seven moves inwards and this encourages people who have seven in their code to respond to matters emotionally. This can lead to bouts of depression complemented with periods of great joy. The symbol of the lake is reflective, which gives these people the ability to reflect other peoples' characters back at them. When the weather is calm, the lake is deep and passive, illustrating that person's ability to hold emotions inside. However, on the rare occasions when the individual becomes upset, he or she reacts quickly and forcefully.

Seven represents the youngest daughter, someone who is traditionally seen as playful, youthful and with a carefree spirit. Seven is therefore a vivacious and light-hearted ki energy. Often, people with this nine ki month number (and to a lesser extent, year number) have the ability to be extremely charming. One of the ways someone with seven ki energy succeeds in life is by using his or her charm, along with the ability to remain focussed on the end result. People with number seven ki energy like to have fun and can be criticised for not taking things seriously.

The trigram for number seven has two yang lines at the bottom with a yin line above them. This depicts a calm, passive surface with a strong yang foundation beneath. The trigram symbolises a more yang nature that sometimes has difficulty moving forward.

PERSONAL QUALITIES

Carefree
Charming
Motivated by material gain
Charismatic
Youthful
Romantic
Sexual
Stylish
Focussed on end results
Pleasure loving

POSSIBLE CAREERS

Business person
Counsellor
Banker
Accountant
Stockbroker
Entertainer
Night club owner
Jeweller

TIMING

Being more financially aware
Feeling more content
Starting a new relationship
Starting a new business
Signing contracts that bring in greater wealth
Having fun
Feeling more romantic
Creating a sense of style
Lacking motivation
Feeling depressed

Favourable for those with year numbers 1, 2, 5, 6, 7 and 8.
9 might have problems with romance and finance.

mountain

soil

north-east

night to dawn
(01.00–05.00)

winter to spring

january & february

youngest son

The number eight is associated with mountain ki energy, which represents the night progressing to dawn and winter turning into spring. To feel this ki energy, you would need to go out before sunrise to a quiet location as winter changes to spring. Ideally, you would be surrounded by mountains and rocks, with a strong, cold north-easterly wind blowing towards you. If you were in such an environment you would become aware of nature changing as it prepares for the new day. The strong, cold wind would be refreshing and stimulating and you would find it easier to possess the clarity you require to renew your sense of purpose in life. You would also find it easier to think of ways to take new initiatives so that situations could work in your favour. If you walked up the mountain, you would be more likely to receive quick flashes of information that would help you see into your own future.

If your number code consists of eight, your prevailing ki energy gives you access to a deeper, inner knowledge that will help you to be more intuitive. This ki energy is also clean, clear, hard, sharp and piercing – qualities that are all ideal for making sudden changes. A good example of this type of energy would be the way a shoal of fish suddenly changes direction in what seems to be a split second. The same quality allows a person with this nine ki number to make snap decisions and seize opportunities before others can react to them.

Someone with eight as his or her nine ki year number will succeed in life by moving forwards into new situations and new opportunities that make the most of his or her skills. However, there is a tendency to find it hard to let go, relax or let someone else win, which can lead to overwork.

Striking exteriors
Just like the spire of a church, people who have eight in their code of numbers have a sharp and cutting aspect to their personality.

Reaching the top

People who have the number eight in their code are highly motivated and, once they achieve their goals, gain a certain clarity of mind.

North-east is the direction that is associated with nine ki number eight; the period between winter and spring is the related season. The number eight therefore has an energy that pertains to a time associated with a seed sprouting its roots and establishing itself in the surrounding soil. Such a transformation from being self-contained to fighting to become established gives someone with this nine ki year or month number an energy that is competitive, together with a strong will to win. This quality can also make people highly self motivated. In the extreme, the nine ki number eight has an energy that might make a person seem greedy and calculating. Similarly, the action of developing from a seed to a life force that relies on its environment makes people with this nine ki number outgoing and sociable. However, when faced with difficulties, there is a tendency to move onto new things or change the situation, rather than work through and resolve the problem.

The symbol of a mountain for this number is a reflection of its energy being hard with a sharp exterior, but containing a softer interior. The piercing sharp aspect can lead people to be critical and cutting on the surface, especially those who have eight for their nine ki month number.

Eight represents the youngest son, someone who is traditionally seen as playful, youthful and sometimes accustomed to being spoilt. People with eight as their nine ki year or month number can be used to getting their own way. They often have a boyish, charming way of doing this, which means they can get what they want without upsetting others. The trigram has a yang line with yin lines below. This depicts the hard, sharp surface at the earth's crust covering the fluid and soft molten lava below.

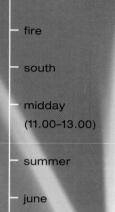

- fire

- south

- midday
  (11.00–13.00)

- summer

- june

- middle daughter

The number nine is associated with fire ki energy and also represents the midday and summer. To feel this ki energy, you would have to go out in the middle of the day in the middle of the summer. Ideally, you would be surrounded by colourful flowers in full bloom. As you stood still, you would be aware of the heat, colour and activity. Summer is the time when everything in nature has come to life and is there to be noticed. Therefore, in such an environment the overriding impression would be of ki energy expanding in every direction. This energy is conducive to being expressive, emotional and passionate and encourages you to feel like going out, seeing things and meeting people. The bright, fiery nature of this energy makes it easier to be visible, so the nine ki number nine helps people to achieve public recognition.

Nine is a ki energy that helps you to feel and express your emotions so if you have this ki energy in your number code, you are more likely to make decisions based on how you feel at the time. You are stimulated both emotionally and mentally, with much of your life being more emotionally led. It is also a very quick energy that helps you react promptly to ideas, and this can keep you at the forefront of changes in fashion. These qualities of a sharp wit and intelligence can impress others. People with this ki

Fun in the sun
A vivacious and sociable nature characterises people with the number nine in their code.

An explosive quality
People who have nine in their code tend to express themselves in an emotional manner.

PERSONAL QUALITIES

Emotional
Sharp wit
Reacts quickly
Passionate
Social
Noticeable
Fiery
Proud

POSSIBLE CAREERS

Prosecution lawyer
Sales person
Public relations person
Advertising executive
Fashion designer
Public speaker
Comedian
Organiser and host of social events
Actor

TIMING

Expressing more emotion
Receiving public recognition
Becoming more outgoing and sociable
Coming up with new ideas
Able to promote yourself
Winning an award
Achieving success
Being argumentative
Separating from people

Favourable for those with year numbers 2, 3, 5, 8 and 9.
4 should resist temptation to separate and be careful of extreme emotions.

energy tend to be proud and fight to outshine others. Being able to feel proud of those close to them is also important.

As this ki energy relates to the middle of the day, it is easy for someone with this nine ki year energy to become successful in midlife. This would be the time to focus on getting noticed, becoming well known and, if appropriate, being famous for something. People who have nine as their month number will find it is easy to concentrate a great amount of this fiery ki energy on things that feel good or right emotionally. However, it also means that they can find it very hard to start or continue with something if it does not feel right. This can lead to a situation where other people perceive a nine fire ki person as doing things only at a time when he or she feels like doing them. Just as with a fire, such a person's energy will fluctuate easily. A good analogy of this is in the way that a few drops of alcohol can suddenly bring a smouldering fire into flames, whereas a few drops of water will quickly dampen it down. In a similar way, individuals with the number nine in their code will be highly influenced by other people; some of their entourage will raise their energy levels and keep them excited, while others are liable to suffocate them.

The fiery, burning nature of this energy gives people with this nine ki month number an explosive side to their characters. They may lose their tempers very quickly and express their anger with powerful emotions. This type of ki energy makes it hard for these people to relax and they can be bothered easily by small details such as the temperature of a room, the comfort of beds and chairs, or other people's behaviour.

The number nine represents the middle daughter, who is traditionally seen as flamboyant, vivacious and social. The trigram has two active yang lines outside and a flexible yin line inside. This reflects the deeper, hot nature of yang being surrounded by the gaseous yin structure of a flame.

Applying feng shui astrology

Now that you know how to calculate your nine ki numbers and construct and read your birth chart, you can use nine ki astrology to help in three particular areas of your life. These are: choosing the right partner, moving in an auspicious direction and planning important events, such as starting a business or a family, so they occur at the most propitious time.

relationships

By comparing two people's code of nine ki numbers you can use feng shui astrology to help determine the compatibility of a relationship. To do this, first look at your nine ki year number and that of your potential partner, and judge how they mix in terms of ki energy (see pages 14–19 and pages 25–33) and the five elements (see page 10). The nine ki year numbers provide clues as to how you relate on a deeper level and over a longer period of time. Then repeat this process for your nine ki month numbers and your nine ki axis numbers. The month numbers reveal how you communicate with each other and how you get on emotionally. The axis numbers suggest how you might do things or work together.

Comparing numbers

The chart on the right and on the proceeding pages gives a short description of each type of relationship between every nine ki number. I have written it as though the people are in a romantic relationship, but you can interpret the description so that it is appropriate for any

Fulfilling the potential

No relationship is perfect, but you can help yourself by using feng shui astrology to choose a partner who is compatible with your basic personality traits and has the same aims in life.

relationship, whether it is with a member of your family, a business partner or a friend. In each case you should read the full description of the nine ki code numbers on pages 25–33 and the full birth charts found on pages 34–73 so that you get the complete picture of the character of the person in question.

The advantages and disadvantages point out key issues to look for. Ideally, we should all build our relationships on the positive characteristics we can share and minimise exposing each other to more destructive elements. In this respect, the disadvantages may show you how you can avoid spoiling a new relationship. If you are already in a long-term relationship and are experiencing problems, nine ki can help you make a more honest appraisal and resolve your differences by accepting each other's unique characteristics.

Advantages / Disadvantages

Advantages		Disadvantages
You both have a flexible approach to life and enjoy independence, privacy and space. You also respect these qualities in others.	YEAR	You can drift apart and be distant and aloof with each other. You may be tempted to run away if things become difficult.
You like to talk a lot and will both find each other stimulating company. You are affectionate and can easily identify with each other's feelings.	MONTH	You may become too caught up in your own lives. You are not always tolerant and may try to impose your will, which will be fiercely resisted.
You are both easy going and laid back, so are able to adapt to different situations. You are both objective and work well together.	AXIS	Both can worry. Problems between you can drift on without either confronting the situation or acknowledging each other's emotions.

1 & 1

Advantages

Disadvantages

1 & 2

YEAR

Two provides security, stability and realism for one. One helps two be more adventurous. This can become a mother–son type of relationship.

One may find two over-cautious and stifling of one's independent, fluid nature. Two can find one too secretive and exhausting at times.

MONTH

Two is caring, considerate and motherly towards one. One is affectionate, inspiring and sexual towards two.

One can find two slow and predictable, and may eventually become bored. Two can be too critical and negative for one's sensitive nature.

AXIS

Two is practical and down to earth, whereas one can help two go with the flow. You make a successful team of opposites.

One will find two structured and rigid. Two's methodical way of working may be distracted by one's worrying.

1 & 3

YEAR

One enjoys three's dynamic and go-ahead attitude, while three appreciates one's independent spirit and ability to be objective.

One may find living with three too stressful and crave peace and quiet. Three could find it hard to understand one's fluid and spiritual side.

MONTH

One likes three's active mind and direct nature. Three finds one stimulating and lively company. One helps three look at the big picture.

One may not tolerate three's impatience or bursts of anger. Three could find one talks too much without enough action.

AXIS

One finds three's enthusiasm infectious and enjoys his or her positive approach to life. Three benefits from one's objectiveness and vision.

Three's inclination to rush ahead will frustrate one, while three may find it hard to cope with one's easy going, laid back attitude.

1 & 4

YEAR

One's flexible approach to life suits four's creative instincts. Both four and one like to move forwards and enjoy being creative.

One could find four too caught up in his or her imagination and unable to let go. Four can find it hard to accept one's desire for independence.

MONTH

You are able to respect each other's sensitive side. Four finds one stimulating and talkative but he or she can exert a calming influence on one.

Four could find one self-obsessed at times, and one may feel frustrated by four's dreamy side. Both are sensitive, which may cause upsets.

AXIS

Four's persistence and tenacity teams well with one's deeper power and superficial calm. You should enjoy each other's company.

One may find it hard to cope with four's impatient approach to work, while four may find one too laid back at times.

1 & 5

YEAR

One finds it easy to follow in the wake of five's power. When five is enjoying being the centre of attention, one retains clarity and purpose.

One may find five overwhelming, preferring to spend more time away from him or her. Five could find one elusive and secretive.

MONTH

Both one and five are potentially changeable and, for this reason, their relationship is best kept exciting and dynamic.

Five can be too confrontational and controlling for the independent, sensitive one. Five will find it hard to penetrate one's mysterious side.

AXIS

Although very different, you can work well as a team by combining your opposing but complementary talents.

Five will want to get everything out in the open and take the initiative, whereas one is happy to sit back and see what happens.

Advantages

Disadvantages

Advantages		Disadvantages

One uses six's sense of structure and organisation as a platform to achieve more. Six's intuitive side enjoys one's spiritual nature.

YEAR

One could find six domineering and controlling, while six may find one hard to understand and feel he or she is running away from six.

One feels secure with six, admiring his or her dignity, while six welcomes one's exuberant nature. Both have a sense of humour.

MONTH

One is fluid and this may disrupt six's sense of organisation. Six's structured nature and lack of emotional expression can stifle one.

Six has a methodical approach to planning. One appreciates this forethought and helps six to be more flexible.

AXIS

One can find six's thorough preparation boring. Six may find one a difficult and sometimes inaccessible team player.

1 & 6

One likes seven's ability to be playful and have fun increasing wealth. One's happy-go-lucky attitude helps seven to ride the changes.

YEAR

Seven feels difficulties should be tackled together, while one prefers dealing with things independently. One can find seven irresponsible.

You can both be entertaining speakers. Seven adds sparkle to one's creative mind and enjoys one's sharp wit. You share a stimulating sex life.

MONTH

You are sensitive and could easily feel hurt by each other. Seven could seem childish at times, while one could appear self-obsessed.

Seven helps one focus on the end result of a project, while one is more attentive to the process of arriving there.

AXIS

Seven can play around too much and lose motivation, while one will tend to worry about the relationship and feel insecure.

1 & 7

Eight prefers to take the direct route, while one is more flexible. At times you are in harmony, at other times you could not be further apart.

YEAR

One may not understand eight's enthusiasm to take what he or she wants from life. Eight will feel one lets certain aspects of life drift by.

Although opposites, you can both be stimulating and enjoy a dynamic relationship. Having your own interests and activities helps this.

MONTH

One may feel eight is calculating and selfish whereas eight can find one condescending and aloof. You know how to hurt each other.

Eight's competitive, direct nature may improve one's motivation. One can help eight to consider the options before rushing ahead.

AXIS

Eight may feel he or she is doing all the work while one watches. One can feel eight rushes ahead, selfishly taking the opportunities.

1 & 8

A dynamic relationship to which one brings peace and tranquillity, while nine counterbalances this with passion and emotion.

YEAR

One may find nine's energy changes too easily and is too dramatic, whereas nine could find one too distant and reserved.

You both enjoy lively communication and find it easy to relate to each other emotionally. Never a dull moment in this relationship.

MONTH

Nine can find one's talkative nature tiring. One can lose patience with nine's desire to express and possibly exaggerate his or her emotions.

One brings clarity of thought to the partnership, while nine establishes social contacts and is excellent at self-promotion.

AXIS

Nine can steal the limelight and blow his or her own trumpet, but he or she may find it hard to figure out one's plans.

1 & 9

Advantages

Disadvantages

2 & 2

You are both able to enjoy an easy, steady pace through life, concentrating on the quality of your activities.	**YEAR**	You may get bored with each other or feel stuck in a routine and crave greater stimulation and excitement.
You are both caring, considerate and understanding. You can depend on each other and would enjoy bringing up a family together.	**MONTH**	Familiarity can breed contempt and you may take each other for granted. You could start looking for more exciting company.
You share a realistic but cautious approach to life and would find it satisfying to do practical activities together.	**AXIS**	Your relationship can lack spontaneity and passion. Although effective in many ways, it may not be emotionally rewarding.

2 & 3

Three likes two's ability to create stability in home and family life, whereas two benefits from three's drive and ambition.	**YEAR**	Three may find two slow and feel that he or she is being held back. Three's desire to rush ahead in different directions is unsettling for two.
Three benefits from two's caring, motherly nature and practical outlook, while two is stimulated by three's dynamism.	**MONTH**	Three can find that two is dependent and clingy, and two may feel that three is unsympathetic and, at times, uncaring.
Three has new ideas and starts new projects easily. Two has high standards, and ensures that plans are executed practically.	**AXIS**	Two can seem over cautious, negative and conservative. Three may be too unrealistic, impatient and frustrated.

2 & 4

Four's sensitive nature appreciates two's motherly, kind and caring side. You both avoid confrontation and seek harmony.	**YEAR**	Two may feel that four lacks the patience to do things properly. Two can be too indecisive and slow for four.
Four enjoys two's considerate side and four stretches two's imagination. You can disagree and actually enjoy the discussion.	**MONTH**	When provoked, two can be too critical and negative for four's sensibilities. Four can be too vague, superficial and dreamy at times.
Two finds four's imagination and stream of ideas stimulating, while four appreciates two's ability to take an idea and enhance it.	**AXIS**	It can be hard to combine four's creativity with two's practicality. Four may be too persistent and override two's ideas.

2 & 5

Two adds stability to five's life, while five brings the power to the relationship. They will both enjoy the harmony of building a life together.	**YEAR**	Two can be upset by five's tendency to make sudden changes and take risks. Five may find two's outlook too negative.
Five enjoys two's attention and is happy for two to be motherly. Two likes five's strength and ability to make powerful decisions.	**MONTH**	Two may find five tiring, self-obsessed and too confrontational. At times, two could be over dependent on five.
You can both be practical and down to earth. Five is keen to tackle bigger projects, while two knows how to make plans work.	**AXIS**	Two will be more cautious and resist five's passion for risk. Five may find it hard to work within two's restrictions.

Advantages

Disadvantages

Advantages		Disadvantages	
You both have a mature attitude to life and respect each other's values. You take each other's thoughts and feelings seriously.	**YEAR**	Two may find it hard to confront six's controlling and overbearing behaviour. Two can be too indecisive for six.	**2 & 6**
Six's authority and organisation reassures two. Two is softer and melts six's seriousness. This can become a mother and father relationship.	**MONTH**	You both can be too serious and lack fun in your relationship. You may crave greater stimulation and excitement at times.	
You are both serious about work. Six's planning ability and two's talents in execution can make you a powerful and successful team.	**AXIS**	Two may resent six's tendency to take over a situation, but six could feel that two lacks the strength to take the initiative.	

Seven often enjoys two's more motherly nature and basks in the warmth of this attention. Two finds seven a playful companion.	**YEAR**	Two can find seven too playful, childish and even lazy. Two can sometimes seem too serious and overly concerned with practicalities.	**2 & 7**
You have mutual pleasures and sex is a source of joy for both of you. You have a harmonious relationship and you feel comfortable together.	**MONTH**	Two can be too critical for seven's more fragile emotions, whereas seven's charms and pursuit of pleasure can provoke jealousy in two.	
Seven adds creative style to a project and focusses on the end result. Two possesses the practical ability to make it work.	**AXIS**	Seven could feel held back by two's natural caution. Two may think that seven is not pulling his or her weight.	

You are both home lovers and value friendships and family life. You often find many areas of common interest.	**YEAR**	Eight is more action-orientated and may take risks that two does not feel comfortable with. Two may come second to eight's projects.	**2 & 8**
Eight can be fun, youthful and playful, whereas two is more responsible and practical. You may have a mother and son type of relationship.	**MONTH**	Two may resent having to take responsibility for things, while eight may eventually get tired of being restrained.	
At times, eight will want to surge ahead and seize an opportunity, while two will tend to follow, tying up all the loose ends.	**AXIS**	Eight is more prone to making mistakes and will be criticised for this. Two's caution may irritate the risk-taking eight.	

Nine brings spontaneity, excitement and an outgoing attitude to the partnership. Two helps nine feel more steady, practical and stable.	**YEAR**	It can be hard for two to cope with nine's changes in mood and enthusiasm. Nine will feel drained by any criticism or negativity.	**2 & 9**
Two thrives on nine's fiery, emotional nature, and nine feels secure with two. Nine's generous side complements two's caring temperament.	**MONTH**	Nine can be explosive and hurtful if his or her pride is hurt, while two knows exactly how to dent nine's lion-sized ego.	
Nine makes useful social contacts and is good at promoting his or her projects. Two is better at developing long-term relationships.	**AXIS**	Two may find nine's approach to work rather chaotic and emotionally led, while nine will not always be willing to wait for two.	

Advantages

Disadvantages

YEAR

You are both ambitious, active and enjoy making things happen. There may be a tendency to be primarily career-orientated.

You can get too caught up in other things and find your relationship falters through neglect. Neither is good at listening to the other.

MONTH

You like doing things together and can live dynamic lives. You are able to communicate directly, clearly and frankly.

You are both impatient and lose your temper with each other at times. You could waste time arguing over who is to.blame for a problem.

AXIS

You will enjoy each other's enthusiasm and have a positive attitude to work. You both like to get straight to the point.

You can both get bored easily and there is a temptation to quickly move onto new projects, which makes for an unstable team.

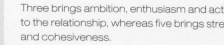

YEAR

Four is romantic, while three is confident and positive. You often lift each other's spirits. Both of you are lovers of action.

You may both become too busy to enjoy your relationship and you tend to blow small differences out of proportion.

MONTH

Four benefits from three's enthusiasm and confidence while three enjoys four's imagination and ability to look at the big picture.

Three can be too frank, direct and sometimes irritable for four's sensitive side, Three may find it hard to tell what four is thinking.

AXIS

You are both positive and like starting projects. With three's technical orientation and four's creativity, you could easily build up a business.

Three is impatient and four can be very persistent. When you disagree, it may be hard to find a way to compromise.

YEAR

Three brings ambition, enthusiasm and activity to the relationship, whereas five brings strength and cohesiveness.

Three may find his or her enthusiasm is blocked by five. Five may find it hard to keep up with three's sometimes negative actions.

MONTH

Three is positive, confident and reassuring and five is magnanimous and influential. A powerful combination when it works.

Three will resist and refuse five the attention that he or she demands. Five will not tolerate three's temper.

AXIS

Both of you have the ability to achieve much. You may tend to work separately, but make a strong team when you find harmony.

There is a risk that your inability to understand each other's way of working will cause a huge division between you.

YEAR

Three has a youthful attitude and is ambitious. Six has a more mature and thoughtful approach to life. A father and son type of relationship.

Three may resist six's tendency to take control, while six may feel a loss of dignity if three becomes irritable or angry.

MONTH

Three is naturally positive and enjoys activity, while six possesses dignity and grace. A success when you appreciate your differences.

You may have a very functional relationship but it could be lacking in affection and passion. You could lose your enthusiasm for sex.

AXIS

Both of you are career-orientated and good at getting things done. Three starts a project and six ensures it is completed successfully.

Three's impatience to get a project off the ground and six's meticulous attention to detail may spark confrontations.

Advantages

Disadvantages

Three's energy and activeness stimulates seven, whereas seven shows three how to have fun, enjoy pleasures and relax.	**YEAR**	Three may feel let down if seven does not match his or her enthusiasm. Seven can find three tiring at times.
Three can have an unusual off-beat manner which seven finds intriguing. Seven can win three over with his or her natural charm.	**MONTH**	Three can be too loud, impatient and irritable for seven's sensibilities. Seven can have bouts of depression, which three will not tolerate.
Three likes to initiate new things, while seven is good at applying his or her energy to turn three's efforts into profit.	**AXIS**	Three can fill his or her time with activities just to keep busy, whereas seven will not be interested unless there is an obvious benefit.

3 & 7

Both of you are career-orientated and value each other's desire to get ahead. You respect each other's successes in business.	**YEAR**	You have little room for love and intimacy. If either of you were to experience failure in life, the relationship would be strained.
You have a dynamic, active relationship where building up your lives provides mutual satisfaction. You are both direct individuals.	**MONTH**	If there is no progress, you can attack each other. Three can become short tempered, while eight will fight back with sharp, biting criticisms.
You make a competitive, ambitious and dynamic team that could take on the best and win, unless you turn on each other.	**AXIS**	You can be too competitive with each other. Without compassion and mutual understanding, the relationship can be tense.

3 & 8

Three likes to rush ahead and build up his or her life. Nine also likes quick results and will bring warmth and passion to the relationship.	**YEAR**	Nine's passion, self-expression and emotional nature may not receive a response from three, while three could find nine too self-centred.
Three's positive, enthusiastic and go-ahead attitude keeps nine's energy high, while nine's natural passion raises three's confidence.	**MONTH**	Three's thundery temper and nine's fiery explosiveness result in lively arguments. The risk is that that such conflict may end in a break up.
With three's drive, ambition and technical ability, and nine's sales ability, social connections and passion, you make an effective team.	**AXIS**	Neither of you is good at making provision for the future or dealing with a situation when things are no longer moving forwards.

3 & 9

Both are creative and imaginative. You stimulate one another and would enjoy seeing your ideas entering the public domain.	**YEAR**	Both of you can stubbornly follow your own path in life, even if that means going separate ways. Resentments can build up in the long-term.
You are comfortable in each other's company and stretch each other mentally. You have an understanding and share a sense of humour.	**MONTH**	You can become irritable and impatient with each other. You both find it hard to let go, being stubborn and holding on to resentments.
You can encourage each other and work well together on creative projects. Both of you are full of ideas and have quick minds.	**AXIS**	You are both tenacious and persistent, but will rarely confront each other. Neither really knows what the other wants; both lack direction.

4 & 4

Advantages   Disadvantages

4 & 5

Advantages		Disadvantages
You can both can be persistent and determined to make things succeed. You enjoy immersing yourselves in work towards a common goal.	YEAR	Once you find you have opposing ideas that are deeply felt, you can both be stubborn with your views, even to the bitter end.
Four can be romantic and imaginative, while five is more solid and down to earth. This is an interesting mix of different energies.	MONTH	Five likes to lay his or her cards on the table and be honest from the outset. Four prefers to keep the cards close to his or her chest.
Five finds four inspiring and stimulating, while four is impressed with five's ability to apply ideas practically and powerfully.	AXIS	Five tends to be confrontational, while four will avoid conflict. Five can become worn down by four's ability to dodge the argument.

4 & 6

Advantages		Disadvantages
Four respects six's wisdom, intuition and apparent experience. Six appreciates this and sees four as youthful, gentle and playful.	YEAR	Four's persistence may frustrate six. In time, six will realise that four is not really easily influenced. Damage will result if four loses respect for six.
Six enjoys four's wealth of ideas and easy-going nature, while four is impressed with six's ability to stick with one idea and develop it carefully.	MONTH	Four can find it difficult to communicate with six, while six will find it hard to know what is going on in four's mind.
Four's creativity stimulates six, whose methodical approach enhances the ideas. Four will often accept six's leadership qualities.	AXIS	Four may become impatient with six's more careful approach. Six may feel that four is rushing ahead and taking unnecessary risks.

4 & 7

Advantages		Disadvantages
You both like to have fun. Four can be attracted to seven's charisma and style, while seven enjoys four's many interests and enthusiasm.	YEAR	You can both become absorbed in your own lives and find that you drift apart. You may not feel a strong bond between you.
You seek harmony and enjoy a warm, comfortable relationship. You share outside interests and may have a very active sex life.	MONTH	You are both sensitive and moody and could easily upset each other. Neither of you will really want to confront the other to sort out problems.
Four is creative, positive and can generate many ideas, This stimulates seven's enthusiasm and he or she can add style and profitability.	AXIS	At times, you will find it hard to understand each other. You can both get lost in your own worlds. It will require effort to work as a team.

4 & 8

Advantages		Disadvantages
You both respect each other's enthusiasm to get on with things. You enjoy building up your lives together and being successful.	YEAR	Both of you can be stubborn, even if this means breaking up. This can become an elder sister and younger brother relationship.
Eight is stimulated by four's ideas, while four can be impressed at eight's ability to get things done. A dynamic relationship of opposites.	MONTH	Eight can be piercing and critical and, although easily hurt, four may hold on to resentments, adding a destructive element to the relationship.
Four provides the creative, artistic and imaginative force, while eight has the business acumen and energy to win new opportunities.	AXIS	Eight can rush into things, making four feel left out. Four can be too vague for eight's quick and sharp approach.

Advantages

Disadvantages

4 & 9

	YEAR	
Four enjoys the excitement of nine's outgoing nature, while nine finds four stimulating. A harmonious brother and sister relationship.	YEAR	Four could find nine overdramatic and too obsessed with his or her own emotions. Nine may crave warmth, passion and generosity.
Four is imaginative, kind and easy going, while nine is passionate, fiery and warm-hearted. You can create a loving and sexual relationship.	MONTH	Nine is critical, while four is sensitive. Both are emotional and are influenced by each other's mood. This may lead to instability.
Nine can enhance four's ideas and take them into the public arena. A mutually stimulating and complementary team.	AXIS	Nine may grab the limelight, leaving four in the shade. Nine will react if his or her pride is hurt. You can both be overemotional.

5 & 5

	YEAR	
Both of you enjoy a mixture of security and adventure.You find each other interesting company and also have a wide circle of friends.	YEAR	Both of you may undergo periods of change, which could take you in different directions. You both hate not being at the centre of things.
You both love intimacy, intrigue and intellectual discussion. You easily relate to each other's emotions and are sympathetic.	MONTH	Both of you can be confrontational and forceful with your ideas. You each need a lot of attention but may be reluctant to reciprocate this.
Each can put up a powerful front and be impressive in meetings or public situations. You can relate to each other's way of doing things.	AXIS	You can both behave as though the world revolves around you. When the pair of you feel like this, there is a real risk of disharmony.

5 & 6

	YEAR	
You are both powerful and can accomplish a great deal. You are even more potent as a team if you appreciate each other's strengths.	YEAR	Five will not readily accept six's desire to take control and five, if provoked, can be confrontational, eventually harming six's dignity.
Five is sturdy and stable, whereas six can be a natural leader. You both enjoy home life and building up financial security together.	MONTH	Six will not always be as sympathetic as five would like, and six may find five too self-centred. Five may feel six is pompous at times.
You make a powerful and effective team. You can impress the rich and famous with your airs of prestige, integrity and reliability.	AXIS	You need to organise your working relationship so that your success is not hindered by damaging power struggles.

5 & 7

	YEAR	
A harmonious relationship in which five enjoys seven's charm and attention, while seven finds five stimulating. You can grow close over time .	YEAR	Seven may resist five's endeavours to make big changes. Five can become jealous if seven focusses his or her charm on others.
You can create a successful and stable partnership. You take small, but lasting, steps towards enhancing your relationship.	MONTH	You can both feel low at times and may need someone overtly positive to help you through. There is also a small risk of stagnation setting in.
Five provides the power and strength behind a project, while seven brings a sense of style, financial insight and forward-looking vision.	AXIS	Seven will not enjoy five's confrontational side. Five may feel that seven is not investing enough energy in the partnership.

Advantages

Disadvantages

Advantages		Disadvantages

You both enjoy power and influence. You are also outgoing and know how to make friends. As a team, you will climb the ladder of success.

YEAR

Both of you are competitive. Five may seek revenge if eight seems to be taking all the rewards. Do not underestimate each other.

You both appreciate the cosy, intimate side of a relationship, while finding each other mentally stimulating. Your sex life can be harmonious.

MONTH

You can both be critical and knowingly hurtful. Your partner may not react, but the pain can remain and lead to permanent resentment.

Eight's raw desire to win, coupled with five's power, can make this a highly motivated and forceful partnership.

AXIS

You must avoid jealousies, petty squabbles and unnecessary criticism to ensure a harmonious long-term relationship.

Nine is emotional and five has a strong desire for change. Five holds the power, while nine has the means to ensure everyone knows it.

YEAR

If the changes and excitement become too much, you may not find the time for intimacy, and you could grow further apart.

Five's power is combined harmoniously with nine's passion, making this an exciting, although perhaps unpredictable, relationship.

MONTH

You may find that arguments become too stressful and spoil your relationship. You both let off steam, which can be dangerous.

Five finds nine a fiery and passionate advocate who can bring five's power into the public domain. This makes for an exciting team.

AXIS

Nine's pride is easily hurt and five may become jealous if nine tries to steal the glory. This could make an explosive partnership at times.

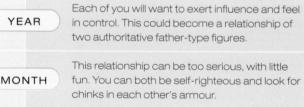

You both respect dignity and integrity as basic values in life. You tend to be responsible and take each other seriously.

YEAR

Each of you will want to exert influence and feel in control. This could become a relationship of two authoritative father-type figures.

Both take life seriously and respect each other for that. Each has an honest way of communicating and enjoys mutual respect.

MONTH

This relationship can be too serious, with little fun. You can both be self-righteous and look for chinks in each other's armour.

Each likes to be well organised and to do things with an air of dignity. Both place an emphasis on getting things right and doing them properly.

AXIS

You may both set excessively high standards for each other and judge by criteria you yourself could not possibly meet.

Six will end up being the father and seven the daughter, which can work well as long as both are happy in these roles. Potentially harmonious.

YEAR

Seven can find six too serious and seek fun with someone else. Six could find seven silly and childish. Six may find seven's moods difficult.

Seven brings a youthful, playful energy to the relationship, while six provides wisdom, security and responsibility.

MONTH

Seven is sensitive to criticism, negativity or lack of appreciation. Six's dignity will be hurt if seven directs his or her charm towards others.

Six can plan ahead, organise and lead, while seven finds ways to bring in money. Both of you enjoy creating material wealth.

AXIS

Seven may not tolerate six's endeavours to take charge of everything. Six will find it difficult to give up control.

Advantages

Disadvantages

YEAR

Eight is mischievous and six more mature. Your partnership could be very successful for career building. Both of you enjoy material success.

Eight can be too impulsive for six who prefers to plan more carefully. The integrity and dignity prized by six may be compromised by eight.

MONTH

Eight is boyish and six more fatherly, so your relationship combines playfulness with responsibility and enthusiasm with wisdom.

Six could be too controlling for the active eight. Six could be judgemental of eight's ethics, while eight may find six tries to block the way forward.

AXIS

The combination of six's wisdom and eight's raw competitive spirit is a recipe for success. Six can organise, while eight wins the work.

Eight may spot the chance of a quick profit, but six may prefer to pass it up and concentrate on doing things right. Neither of you gives in easily.

YEAR

Nine complements six's serious side with passion and excitement. Nine respects six's dignity and wisdom. Both of you have pride.

Six could feel drained by nine's desire to go out and socialise. Nine may feel that six is not appreciative enough. Both of you are stubborn.

MONTH

Six can provide reassurance for the emotional nine. Nine helps six to be more free and open. You both find each other attractively curious.

Six will dislike any sign that nine cannot control his or her emotions, while nine could find six too controlling, dominant and serious.

AXIS

Six is good at planning and organisation, while nine likes to go out and network. You take pride in what you do and share a belief in integrity.

Nine can be too emotionally led for six's logical outlook. Any hint that nine is out of control will unnerve six. Nine will lose passion if restricted.

YEAR

You enjoy seeking pleasure and having fun. You like building up your material wealth together and creating a positive vision for the future.

You can both become irresponsible and go through phases of extravagance. You may encourage each other to go too far.

MONTH

You can both be charismatic, entertaining and charming. You feel relaxed and comfortable in each other's company. Fun and playful in bed.

You are both sensitive, moody and can even get depressed. Another seven is not always the best person to lift the depression.

AXIS

You are both financially aware and enjoy finding ways to increase your income. You understand each other and can both charm other people.

When too comfortable, you can lose motivation and pursue individual pleasures. The temptation to stop work and have fun may be too great.

YEAR

You both have a playful streak and seek out fun and entertainment. You enjoy building up your material wealth together.

Eight can become a workaholic, and seven is happy to let eight do the work. Eight is stubborn, and seven sensitive. Both can be irresponsible.

MONTH

You can challenge each other and lead each other on to greater heights. Seven is more romantic, while eight is more motivated.

Eight can be too direct and critical for seven's more sensitive nature. Seven's charming manner with others can make eight jealous.

AXIS

A youthful partnership, where eight's will to win and seven's ability to focus on the end result can bring success. You should have fun.

Eight may be too competitive and keen to forge ahead and grab the glory. Eight may feel jealous if seven does less work, but still attains the prize.

Advantages

Disadvantages

Advantages		Disadvantages
Both of you are people-orientated. Nine enjoys seven's calm, reflective nature, whereas seven finds nine spontaneous and exciting.	**YEAR**	Seven can scorn nine's attempts to boast, finding him or her too self-centred. Nine may be too critical for seven's sensitive nature.
Seven enjoys nine's generous, passionate and big-hearted love, lapping up the attention. Nine finds seven a fun and entertaining playmate.	**MONTH**	Seven may find it hard to cope with nine's mood swings and nine will find it hard to keep his or her spirits up if seven becomes depressed.
Nine can generate attention and attract publicity, while seven concentrates on the end result and profits. Mutually stimulating.	**AXIS**	Seven's sensitivity, coupled with nine's ego, risks emotional upset. If nine is explosive, seven will not know how to react and may withdraw.

Advantages		Disadvantages
Both of you like to compete and work hard, making this a relationship that can revolve around careers. You like to play and have fun.	**YEAR**	You may forget to relax and spend time really getting to know each other. You may both wonder how committed the other is.
You both like to work hard and play hard. This relationship is likely to be fast and dynamic, without any dull moments.	**MONTH**	Both of you can be critical and tend to blame each other, making it a stressful relationship. You may not make time for romance.
You are hard-working and dedicated, with a will to win, This can make a successful partnership, as long as you do not turn on each other.	**AXIS**	You may attack each other, rather than sort out problems. You can motivate each other too much, leading to an unbalanced lifestyle.

Advantages		Disadvantages
Both of you are outgoing and enjoy having a large circle of friends and being well known in it. This relationship should be busy and active.	**YEAR**	You can be critical of each other. Nine can feel eight takes everything for him-or herself, while nine can be self-centred and easily stressed.
Nine brings passion, emotion and drama to the relationship, while eight brings playfulness, youthful energy and a sense of liveliness.	**MONTH**	Nine can feel his or her natural generosity is being abused. Nine may question eight's long-term intentions. Nine can steal the limelight.
A high energy partnership built on eight's desire to get ahead and nine's enthusiasm to become well known. You will be mutually stimulating.	**AXIS**	Eight may compete with nine and feel jealous if nine gets more attention. Nine may find it hard to keep up. You may attack each other.

Advantages		Disadvantages
Both of you enjoy an outgoing relationship. You are spontaneous together and feel a sense of harmony. An emotionally satisfying relationship.	**YEAR**	Your fiery natures can make for a stressful relationship. The risk is that you will separate at times of high emotion.
You are both warm-hearted, expressive, loving, passionate and generous. You feel you have someone who really understands you.	**MONTH**	Your passion can make you highly strung, leading to frequent arguments. You can explode once too often and have to part.
Both of you are great networkers. You can inspire colleagues and make a wonderful sales team. You can easily attract attention.	**AXIS**	Both of you are proud and like attention. Problems may arise if you injure each other's pride. You can both be emotionally led.

timing events

Every year, month and day has its own prevailing ki energy, called ambient energy. This energy can subtly affect your own year ki energy. For example, when you try to perform a task at a time when ambient ki energy is auspicious for you, it is likely to be easier to accomplish. But when the ki energy is working against you, you will find that success is more difficult or the task takes much more effort. If you repeatedly try to achieve a goal at a time when the prevailing ki energy is detrimental to your own ki energy, you are most likely to give up and feel a failure. This can colour the perception you have of yourself and may ultimately result in diminished expectations. The key to avoiding this negative cycle is to look at the ki energy of the coming months and years, and plan ahead so that you can use this energy to your advantage.

The influence ambient ki energy has over you depends on the strength of your own ki energy at the time. If you are young and full of vitality, ambition and confidence, you will find it easier to succeed regardless of the prevailing ki energy. However, if you are already experiencing difficulties or you're not at your peak, you are more likely to notice the benefits of doing things at a time when the ambient ki energy is compatible with your goal. The principle for everyone is to ensure that the ambient ki energy is working for you rather than against you. This will help you do more in life with less effort.

Prevailing year ki energy

The most influential ambient ki energy is that of the year. If you look at the year charts on the following page, you will notice that every year, your own nine ki year number is in a different position. The ki energy of each position on the chart will influence you in a different way, making it easier for you to achieve certain things at certain times. For example, if your nine ki year number is four, it is easier for you to start new projects, such as a business or career, when four is in the eastern direction (as it is in the year 2003). Once you know which direction your nine ki year number occupies in any given year, you can plan new ventures so that you have the optimum chance of success.

The year charts are referred to by their central number and each year, the number at the centre of the chart descends by one. For example, the year 2000 is a nine year, 2001 an eight year, 2002 a seven

An addition at the right time
Feng shui astrology can help you plan the most important changes in your life, such as having a baby, to maximise your chances of health and happiness.

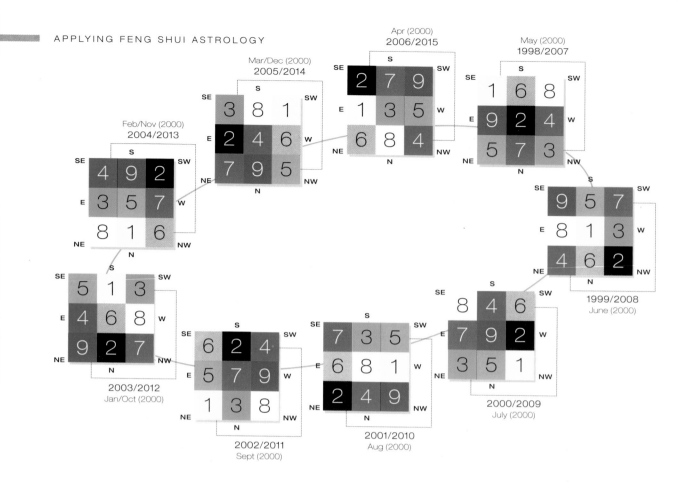

The flow of year ki energy

There are nine different ways ambient year ki energy can flow. This pattern repeats itself every nine years so that the flow of ki energy for the year 2000 is the same as for the year 2009.

The flow of month ki energy

Because there are 12 months each year but the month ki energy changes every nine months, some months will share the same chart. For example, in the year 2000 January, February and March share the same charts as October, November and December 2000 respectively. The months indicated on the diagram above are correct for the year 2000.

year and so on. The numbers revolve round the charts in a specific sequence. In 1999, for example, number one is in the centre of the chart. It then moves northwest in the year 2000, then west in 2001, northeast in 2002, south in 2003, north in 2004, southwest in 2005, east in 2006 and southeast in 2007. The other numbers move around the chart in the same way.

The months descend in a similar pattern to the years so that February 2000 will be a five month, March 2000 a four month, April 2000 a three month and so on (see chart above). To find the number of any month, look at the chart on page 20. This will also provide you with the exact dates and times the nine ki months begin. For a quick calculation, see 'Calculating your month number' on page 17.

The ki energy of each year will have a more powerful effect on your own ki energy than the more subtle prevailing ki energy for the months. The most powerful influence in any year will be when the prevailing year and month ki energy are the same. If you are planning to get married and your nine ki year number is eight, the year 2000 is a good year because eight is in the south-east direction of that year chart. South-eastern ki energy will also be the prevailing ki energy in July, so this month will be a particularly auspicious time.

Entering phases

The direction that your nine ki year number occupies on a year chart is known as a 'phase', so if your nine ki year number is to the west of the year chart, you will be in the western phase. This phase determines the influences on your life during the year in question. Remember, because the feng shui calendar begins around 4 February, if you are planning an event in January 2003, you need to refer to the year chart that relates to 2002 (the seven year chart). See the timing box on pages 77–93 for further information on how you will feel in each phase and which nine ki year numbers will benefit most.

There are two situations where you need to be particularly careful. The first and most significant is when your year number is opposite the powerful force of five. In the year 2000, five is to the north and four, situated in the south, is opposite five. If your nine ki year number is four, you are likely to feel blocked, stressed and out of control if you try to move forwards. It is therefore wiser in 2000 to position yourself so that opportunities come to you and to stay with things with which you are already secure and confident.

The second situation in which you need to be particularly careful is when your nine ki year number is opposite its normal position in the standard 'magic square' chart (see page 13). In the year 2000, seven is in the east, opposite its normal western position in the magic square. For people with the year number seven, this means that events may not turn out as planned, so it is better to be prepared for the unexpected.

You also need to be wary when your nine ki year number is at the centre of the chart (known as the phase of five). When your year number is in the phase of five you are more susceptible to sudden and unpredictable changes. If you initiate radical changes during this phase you run the risk of situations getting out of control – small problems can quickly develop into bigger ones – so it is better just to go with the flow and ride the changes as they happen. In this sense, when you are in the phase of five, it is a useful time to let opportunities come to you. You will also need to check whether you are in your disharmonious phase; see page 114 before embarking on any life-changing events.

Continuity of ki energy

When planning ahead with nine ki astrology it is important to think in terms of several years to get the full benefit. To take one year in isolation and expect the full effect of that ki energy is not realistic. Ideally, you will enter each new phase from a position of power having used the previous phase to its full effect. If you enter the west phase with severe financial problems, for example, this will detract from your ability to

Getting married

By discovering what phase your nine ki year number occupies in any given year, you can plan ahead so that your wedding day falls at the most auspicious time for both you and your partner.

make it a financially prosperous year. The idea is to give yourself about three or four years to make a powerful change. If you want to start a new business in the east phase, for example, you should use the preceding north and south-west phases to lead into the east. The north phase would be useful for thinking about your business ideas in a more objective manner while keeping your options open. The south-west would then be helpful for research, gaining practical experience and for finding useful long-term contacts. With all this in place, your chances of making a success of your new venture during the east phase will be enhanced. You also will have the following phase of the south-east to help expand and establish your business.

There are two major times of change in each nine-year cycle: during the phase of five and when your number moves from the south of the chart to the north. This leaves two four-year periods during which you can build up continuity in your life. The first is north, south-west, east and south-east. The second is north-west, west, north-east and south. Sometimes it is helpful to plan ahead in four-year chunks using this system.

Couples, families and teams

If you want to know the most auspicious time for an event that involves other people, you need to decide whose year number is more important. Ideally, it is the person who has the largest influence and who is most likely to determine the fortunes of the others. A couple preparing a wedding or thinking about starting a family needs to take equal account of both partners' year numbers. Similarly, in a business partnership where each person has equal ownership and control, you would ideally find a month and year where all are in powerful positions. A large company will use the year number of the chairperson, chief executive or managing director to work out when to make major changes because this person's decisions will influence every one else in the company.

Scheduling life events

The charts on the following pages list the phases or directions for each event in order of preference, so to have the greatest chance of success, you should choose a time when your year number is in the first direction. The next best situation would be if your year number is in the equivalent month phase. For example, if you want to start a family, pick a time when your year number is the northern phase. If you have the year or month number five, the year 2000 would be a good year, and July would be a good month, because year number five will be in the north.

Timing family events

Parents are the carers of children and their ability to cope with difficulties have a bearing on their children's lives. This is why the parents' nine ki numbers should be considered first and foremost.

STUDYING AND TRAINING

North This phase is associated with good memory, so it is an ideal period in which to learn new skills.

North-east The ki energy in this phase is beneficial for acquiring knowledge and developing a quick-thinking, sharp mind. There is a competitive edge to this phase which gives you increased motivation to pass exams.

East This phase is conducive to studying more digitally based subjects such as electronics, computer software, logic systems and futuristic technical subjects.

South-east The creative and imaginative aspect of this phase is helpful for studying subjects such as travel, art, languages, film, media, publishing and photography.

South The fiery ki energy of this phase is mentally stimulating and therefore good for any situation where you need intellectually to master a new subject.

South-west The energy here is settling and associated with research and concentration.

West This phase is associated with enjoyment, so ensure you study a subject you enjoy.

North-west This phase is good for being organised and structured in terms of applying yourself. It is helpful for self discipline.

STARTING A NEW CAREER

East You will feel confident, enthusiastic and ambitious while in this phase, so it is a good time to begin a new career. You will have a rapid start and become established in a short space of time.

West This phase is associated with financial awareness so any projects relating to money may turn out to be lucrative for you.

North-west Dignity, responsibility and authority are all related to this phase, so it is an ideal time to seek a promotion or take on a new management role.

South-east This is the perfect phase to take on something new that can lead to future prosperity.

South This is another good phase for gaining a promotion or looking for a new job because it is associated with creating a good impression and being noticed.

North-east This phase is associated with being more competitive and motivated. However, it could make a career change more stressful and prone to conflicts.

Centre, north and south-west The ki energy in the centre phase is too unstable to be a first choice; the north is too quiet; and the south-west is too slow.

RELATIONSHIPS

East You will be enthusiastic to do things with your lover in this phase, but you may be more irritable and less inclined to listen.

South-east You will tend to seek harmony in your relationship and are likely to feel positive about things. At times, though, you could be rather persistent, even devious.

Centre You will enjoy being the centre of attention. You may be indecisive with regard to your feelings for your lover.

North-west A helpful phase to develop mutual respect and set your relationship on a more serious and permanent footing. You could, however, be a little condescending.

West A good phase to be more romantic and have fun with your lover. Physical pleasure will be more important. You may not take your partner seriously, though.

North-east This can be a playful, boisterous phase in which you do a lot together. You may feel more like fighting with your lover and are better able to stand your ground.

South A passionate, warm and generous phase. You may feel argumentative and could react strongly if your pride is hurt. Big bust ups followed by emotional reunions are likely.

North An ideal phase for sex, affection and exploring each other's deeper side.

South-west You are likely to feel cosy, comfortable and intimate with your lover. You could lose the excitement and spontaneity in your relationship.

GETTING PROMOTED

North-west This is the most advantageous phase as you are in a ki energy that is associated with leadership. It will be easier to win respect and present yourself as someone who can take extra responsibility in your stride.

South This is a good phase to promote yourself and attract attention. However, as you are in the north phase the following year, it would be better to gain a promotion early on in the south phase so you have sufficient time to become well established.

East This phase is associated with ambition and is conducive to seeking new opportunities to improve your position. However, the easiest way to gain a promotion could be to move to another company.

North-east This is a competitive phase associated with identifying new opportunities and acting upon them immediately. However, others will feel you are rushing ahead too quickly.

South-east This is a positive phase to make a harmonious transition into a more senior role.

North, south-west, west and centre The ki energy in the north is too quiet; south-western is too slow; and western is considered too immature. The central ki energy is powerful but the results can be unpredictable.

RUNNING A BUSINESS

East The strong energy of this phase is associated with new growth, so will help a new business get off to a flying start. A time for expansion.

South-east A good time for marketing and building up the business internationally.

Centre A period of flux. The business may have to adapt to a changing environment.

North-west A time for management restructuring. Stronger leadership will mean the development of far-reaching long-term plans.

West The business will reach a stage in which profitability can be increased and finance raised, for example through a stock market flotation.

North-east In this phase, the business will be more competitive and quick to react to short-term opportunities.

South The business will be in a good position to promote itself in this phase and increase sales through PR and advertising.

North This is a reflective phase, during which the business will look inwards and concentrate on its own internal systems with the aim of becoming more flexible.

South-west The business will forge closer and more harmonious long-term relationships with its employees and clients.

GETTING MARRIED

South-east The ki energy in this phase is positive, tenacious, persistent and harmonious so bodes well for a long relationship.

West This phase is related to contentment and will ensure you begin your life together with a sense of fun. It encourages a playful marriage that will be pleasurable. However, it is not ideal if you are immature or childish in a relationship.

North-west and south-west These phases represent the father and mother and will lead to a mature marriage. North-west energy will produce a responsible, respectful and dignified relationship while the south-west will lead to a more family orientated, caring and close relationship.

East This phase is ideal for people who want to enjoy their marriage while still retaining enthusiasm for their careers. You will feel positive, confident and enthusiastic. However, you can become impatient, irritable and short tempered.

North, north-east, south and centre These phases are less desirable. The north is too quiet; the north-east is too competitive and argumentative; the south is very passionate but can encourage arguments and emotional upsets; the centre is too unstable and unpredictable.

BUYING A NEW HOME

South-west, centre and north-east These phases are associated with homes and buildings. You will feel enthusiastic and confident about creating a new home.

South-west This phase will encourage you to spend time and energy finding the ideal home.

The centre During this phase you may have difficulty making decisions, although interesting prospects could come your way.

North-east This phase is associated with identifying potentially profitable opportunities.

West This phase is related to finance and you will be in a useful position to arrange a mortgage.

North-west This phase is ideal for considering all your options in a logical manner.

East You will be ambitious, but may rush into decisions too quickly.

South-east This phase can help you make the process more harmonious but you may be too sensitive if things go wrong.

South The emotional energy of this phase will make you base your decision on how the house feels rather than considering other practical factors.

North You will crave an isolated and peaceful home in this phase and will find problems difficult.

When moving, it is important to move in a favourable direction (see pages 118 to 125).

BECOMING SPIRITUAL

North This phase is ideal for healing activities that require convalescence, inner peace or deeper regeneration. If combined with rest and a more relaxed lifestyle, this could be a helpful time to improve your health and recharge your batteries. The inward-looking nature of this ki energy makes it beneficial for spiritual activities such as meditation, chanting and prayer. It is an ideal time to objectively look at your life and you will find it easy to implement any changes.

North-west This phase is related to heaven, making you feel more at ease with spiritual matters. You will also have strong intuitive feelings about what to do with your life.

North-east The quick ki energy associated with this phase makes it good for clarity of thought and flashes of inspiration. This is a good phase for therapy.

South This phase is related to religion and you will find it easy to express your emotions. Therapy can be beneficial although you may get lost in your own feelings.

East and south-east It is harder to focus on spiritual activities during these two phases.

South-west and west The south-west phase is too dependent and the west phase too playful.

Centre The centre phase can be good for spiritual activities as long as they have a steadying effect on your life. However, you could become too fanatical and take them to extremes.

STARTING A FAMILY

North This phase is ideal because you are in harmony with the natural forces that are associated with conception. You will be more content to relax, stay at home and take care of yourself which is important when pregnant.

South-western Motherhood and family harmony are associated with this phase, making it the ideal time to be concentrating on your new baby.

North-west and west These are phases in which your emotions are more in harmony with pregnancy and raising a newborn baby.

East, south-east and south You feel most outgoing during these phases and can feel that pregnancy and a new baby are preventing you from going out. This can lead to resentment

North-east and centre These are less stable phases and not ideally suited to raising a newborn baby. However, while in the north-eastern phase, there is an increased chance of conception.

Disharmonious phases

One final aspect that you need to consider when making major decisions in your life is your disharmonious phase. This is an unsettled period in which you should not do anything of major importance and, in particular, anything that has a lasting influence on your life, such as getting married, starting a business or making a major investment for the future. The disharmonious phase relates to two years, two months and four hours of the day in every 12-year, 12-month or 24-hour cycle, and is determined by your date of birth as follows.

The ancient Chinese calendar is divided up into two cycles. The first is a 10-day cycle in which each day is associated with a yin or yang element, known as the stem. The second is a 12-day cycle in which each day is assigned one of the 12 astrological animals (see page 36), known as the branch. (These same cycles also apply to months and years.) Every ten days, the stem cycle begins again while the remaining two animals complete the branch cycle. This creates a period of change, known as a disharmonious phase, where the harmony of one cycle is broken before a new one begins.

The chart below shows how the two stem and branch cycles work. It can be extended backwards or forwards in time to cover any date simply by repeating the cycle. Working forwards, for example, we can predict that after tree yin comes fire yang and after the boar comes the rat. This means that 19 January 2000 will be a tree yang rat day and so on. The last day of the 20th century in the Western calendar – 31 December 1999 – will be a fire yin snake day.

The chart overleaf will help you identify the two disharmonious animals associated with the stem cycle in which you were born. Locate the square of your birth year. Within that square, look in every coloured box until you find your birth date or the date that most closely precedes it,

Disharmonious phases for 2000

The chart below shows the first eighteen days of the year 2000. The stem cycle begins on 7 January with tree yang and ends on 16 January with water yin. Dog and boar are the two remaining animals at end of the of the stem cycle, and at the beginning of the next. Therefore, anyone born between 7 and 16 January 2000 inclusively will have as their disharmonious phase any hour, day, month or year that is associated with the dog and boar (see the circular chart opposite).

year number attributes

STEM	SOIL		METAL		WATER		TREE		FIRE
	yang	yin	yang	yin	yang	yin	yang	yin	yang
BRANCH									
JAN 2000	1	2	3	4	5	6	7 cycle begins	8	9

and note the colour of the back-ground. Use the colour-coded key at the top of the chart to determine your disharmonious animals. For example, if you were born on 25 April 1965, they would be tiger and rabbit. Once you know your two animals, look at the circular chart on the right to discover the disharmonious times of day, months and years associated with these animals. For example, if your disharmonious phase falls in the dog/boar stem, you need to be more careful between the hours of 19.00 to 23.00 each day, the months of October and November each year and the years 2006 and 2007, as well as further dog and boar years. (To discover which would be dog and boar days you can extend the chart below or buy an appropriate Chinese year calender. For most purposes, however, the influence of the days is small compared to the years.) If you cannot wait until you are in a year when your ki energy is not disharmonious, it becomes more important to ensure that the month and, to lesser extent, the day and hour are favourable.

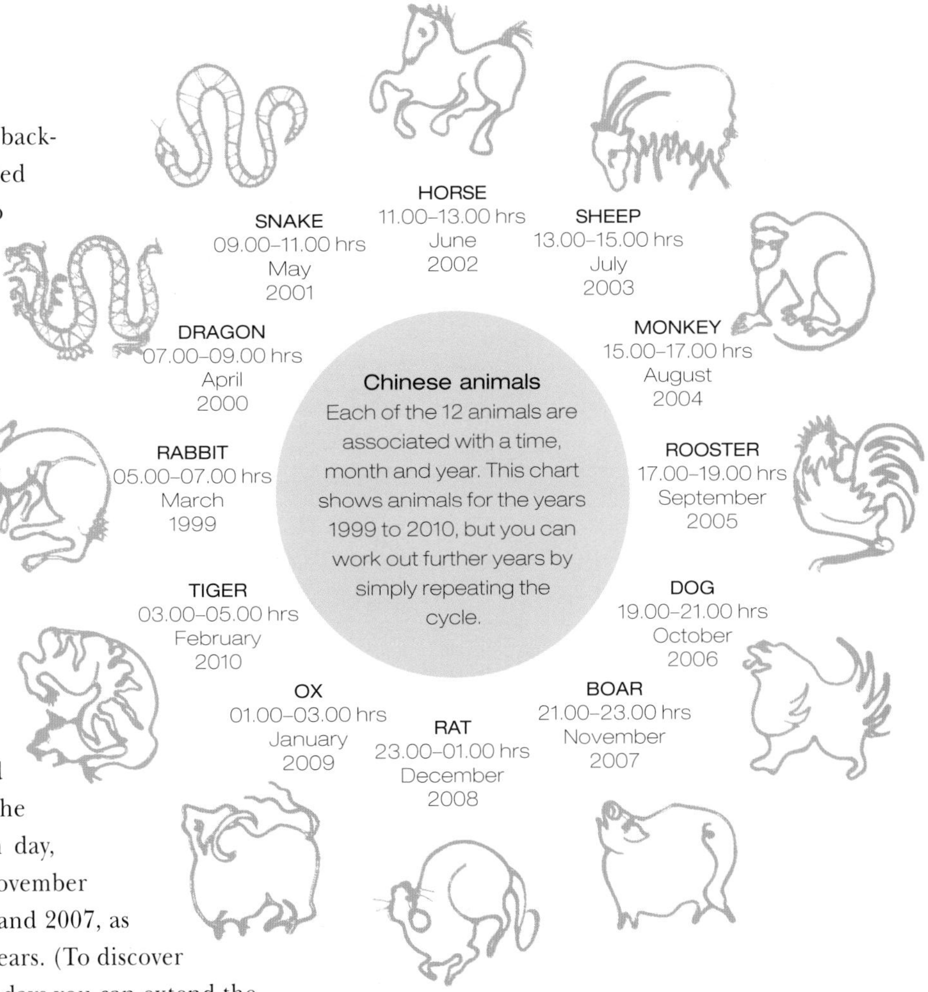

HORSE
11.00–13.00 hrs
June
2002

SNAKE
09.00–11.00 hrs
May
2001

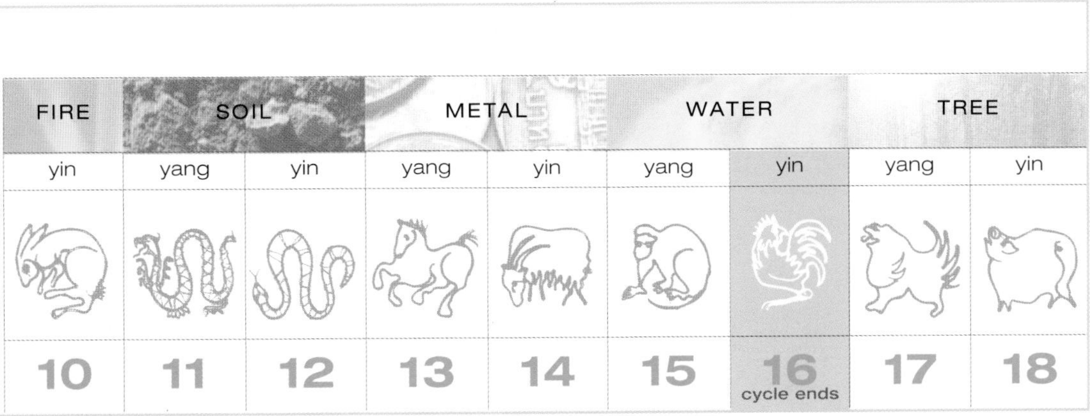

SHEEP
13.00–15.00 hrs
July
2003

DRAGON
07.00–09.00 hrs
April
2000

MONKEY
15.00–17.00 hrs
August
2004

Chinese animals
Each of the 12 animals are associated with a time, month and year. This chart shows animals for the years 1999 to 2010, but you can work out further years by simply repeating the cycle.

RABBIT
05.00–07.00 hrs
March
1999

ROOSTER
17.00–19.00 hrs
September
2005

TIGER
03.00–05.00 hrs
February
2010

DOG
19.00–21.00 hrs
October
2006

OX
01.00–03.00 hrs
January
2009

BOAR
21.00–23.00 hrs
November
2007

RAT
23.00–01.00 hrs
December
2008

FIRE	SOIL		METAL			WATER		TREE	
yin	yang	yin	yang	yin	yang	yin	yang	yin
10	11	12	13	14	15	16 cycle ends	17	18

dog & boar

monkey & rooster

horse & sheep

40	22/1/40, 22/3/40, 21/5/40, 20/7/40, 18/9/40, 17/11/40	11/2/40, 11/4/40, 10/6/40, 9/8/40, 8/10/40, 7/12/40	2/3/40, 1/5/40, 30/6/40, 29/8/40, 28/10/40, 27/12/40	1/2/40, 1/4/40, 31/5/40, 30/7/40, 28/9/40, 27/11/40	21/2/40, 21/4/40, 20/6/40, 19/8/40, 18/10/40, 17/12/40	12/1/40, 12/3/40, 11/5/40, 10/7/40, 8/9/40, 7/11/40
41	16/1/41, 17/3/41, 16/5/41, 15/7/41, 13/9/41, 12/11/41	5/2/41, 6/4/41, 5/6/41, 4/8/41, 3/10/41, 2/12/41	25/2/41, 26/4/41, 25/6/41, 24/8/41, 23/10/41, 22/12/41	26/1/41, 27/3/41, 26/5/41, 25/7/41, 23/9/41, 22/11/41	15/2/41, 16/4/41, 15/6/41, 14/8/41, 13/10/41, 12/12/41	6/1/41, 7/3/41, 6/5/41, 5/7/41, 3/9/41, 2/11/41
42	11/1/42, 12/3/42, 11/5/42, 10/7/42, 8/9/42, 7/11/42	31/1/42, 1/4/42, 31/5/42, 30/7/42, 28/9/42, 27/11/42	20/2/42, 21/4/42, 20/6/42, 19/8/42, 18/10/42, 17/12/42	21/1/42, 22/3/42, 21/5/42, 20/7/42, 18/9/42, 17/11/42	10/2/42, 11/4/42, 10/6/42, 9/8/42, 8/10/42, 7/12/42	1/1/42, 2/3/42, 1/5/42, 30/6/42, 29/8/42, 28/10/42, 27/12/42
43	6/1/43, 7/3/43, 6/5/43, 5/7/43, 3/9/43, 2/11/43	26/1/43, 27/3/43, 26/5/43, 25/7/43, 23/9/43, 22/11/43	15/2/43, 16/4/43, 15/6/43, 14/8/43, 13/10/43, 12/12/43	16/1/43, 17/3/43, 16/5/43, 15/7/43, 13/9/43, 12/11/43	5/2/43, 6/4/43, 5/6/43, 4/8/43, 3/10/43, 2/12/43	25/2/43, 26/4/43, 25/6/43, 24/8/43, 23/10/43, 22/12/43
44	1/1/44, 1/3/44, 30/4/44, 29/6/44, 28/8/44, 27/10/44, 26/12/44	21/1/44, 21/3/44, 20/5/44, 19/7/44, 17/9/44, 16/11/44	10/2/44, 10/4/44, 9/6/44, 8/8/44, 7/10/44, 6/12/44	11/1/44, 11/3/44, 10/5/44, 9/7/44, 7/9/44, 6/11/44	31/1/44, 31/3/44, 30/5/44, 29/7/44, 27/9/44, 26/11/44	20/2/44, 20/4/44, 19/6/44, 18/8/44, 17/10/44, 16/12/44

50	29/1/50, 30/3/50, 29/5/50, 28/7/50, 26/9/50, 25/11/50	18/2/50, 19/4/50, 18/6/50, 17/8/50, 16/10/50, 15/12/50	9/1/50, 10/3/50, 9/5/50, 8/7/50, 6/9/50, 5/11/50	8/2/50, 9/4/50, 8/6/50, 7/8/50, 6/10/50, 5/12/50	28/2/50, 29/4/50, 28/6/50, 27/8/50, 26/10/50, 25/12/50	19/1/50, 20/3/50, 19/5/50, 18/7/50, 16/9/50, 15/11/50
51	24/1/51, 25/3/51, 24/5/51, 23/7/51, 21/9/51, 20/11/51	13/2/51, 14/4/51, 13/6/51, 12/8/51, 11/10/51, 10/12/51	4/1/51, 5/3/51, 4/5/51, 3/7/51, 1/9/51, 31/10/51, 30/12/51	3/2/51, 4/4/51, 3/6/51, 2/8/51, 1/10/51, 30/11/51	23/2/51, 24/4/51, 23/6/51, 22/8/51, 21/10/51, 20/12/51	14/1/51, 15/3/51, 14/5/51, 13/7/51, 11/9/51, 10/11/51
52	19/1/52, 19/3/52, 18/5/52, 17/7/52, 15/9/52, 14/11/52	8/2/52, 8/4/52, 7/6/52, 6/8/52, 5/10/52, 4/12/52	28/2/52, 28/4/52, 27/6/52, 26/8/52, 25/10/52, 24/12/52	29/1/52, 29/3/52, 28/5/52, 27/7/52, 25/9/52, 24/11/52	18/2/52, 18/4/52, 17/6/52, 16/8/52, 15/10/52, 14/12/52	9/1/52, 9/3/52, 8/5/52, 7/7/52, 5/9/52, 4/11/52
53	13/1/53, 14/3/53, 13/5/53, 12/7/53, 10/9/53, 9/11/53	2/2/53, 3/4/53, 2/6/53, 1/8/53, 30/9/53, 29/11/53	22/2/53, 23/4/53, 22/6/53, 21/8/53, 20/10/53, 19/12/53	23/1/53, 24/3/53, 23/5/53, 22/7/53, 20/9/53, 19/11/53	12/2/53, 13/4/53, 12/6/53, 11/8/53, 10/10/53, 9/12/53	3/1/53, 4/3/53, 3/5/53, 2/7/53, 31/8/53, 30/10/53, 29/12/53
54	8/1/54, 9/3/54, 8/5/54, 7/7/54, 5/9/54, 4/11/54	28/1/54, 29/3/54, 28/5/54, 27/7/54, 25/9/54, 24/11/54	17/2/54, 18/4/54, 17/6/54, 16/8/54, 15/10/54, 14/12/54	18/1/54, 19/3/54, 18/5/54, 17/7/54, 15/9/54, 14/11/54	7/2/54, 8/4/54, 7/6/54, 6/8/54, 5/10/54, 4/12/54	27/2/54, 28/4/54, 27/6/54, 26/8/54, 25/10/54, 24/12/54

60	6/2/60, 6/4/60, 5/6/60, 4/8/60, 3/10/60, 2/12/60	26/2/60, 26/4/60, 25/6/60, 24/8/60, 23/10/60, 22/12/60	17/1/60, 17/3/60, 16/5/60, 15/7/60, 13/9/60, 12/11/60	16/2/60, 16/4/60, 15/6/60, 14/8/60, 13/10/60, 12/12/60	7/1/60, 7/3/60, 6/5/60, 5/7/60, 3/9/60, 2/11/60	27/1/60, 27/3/60, 26/5/60, 25/7/60, 23/9/60, 22/11/60
61	31/1/61, 1/4/61, 31/5/61, 30/7/61, 28/9/61, 27/11/61	20/2/61, 21/4/61, 20/6/61, 19/8/61, 18/10/61, 17/12/61	11/1/61, 12/3/61, 11/5/61, 10/7/61, 8/9/61, 7/11/61	10/2/61, 11/4/61, 10/6/61, 9/8/61, 8/10/61, 7/12/61	1/1/61, 2/3/61, 1/5/61, 30/6/61, 29/8/61, 28/10/61, 27/12/61	21/1/61, 22/3/61, 21/5/61, 20/7/61, 18/9/61, 17/11/61
62	26/1/62, 27/3/62, 26/5/62, 25/7/62, 23/9/62, 22/11/62	15/2/62, 16/4/62, 15/6/62, 14/8/62, 13/10/62, 12/12/62	6/1/62, 7/3/62, 6/5/62, 5/7/62, 3/9/62, 2/11/62	5/2/62, 6/4/62, 5/6/62, 4/8/62, 3/10/62, 2/12/62	25/2/62, 26/4/62, 25/6/62, 24/8/62, 23/10/62, 22/12/62	16/1/62, 17/3/62, 16/5/62, 15/7/62, 13/9/62, 12/11/62
63	21/1/63, 22/3/63, 21/5/63, 20/7/63, 18/9/63, 17/11/63	10/2/63, 11/4/63, 10/6/63, 9/8/63, 8/10/63, 7/12/63	1/1/63, 2/3/63, 1/5/63, 30/6/63, 29/8/63, 28/10/63, 27/12/63	31/1/63, 1/4/63, 31/5/63, 30/7/63, 28/9/63, 27/11/63	20/2/63, 21/4/63, 20/6/63, 19/8/63, 18/10/63, 17/12/63	11/1/63, 12/3/63, 11/5/63, 10/7/63, 8/9/63, 7/11/63
64	16/1/64, 16/3/64, 15/5/64, 14/7/64, 12/9/64, 11/11/64	5/2/64, 5/4/64, 4/6/64, 3/8/64, 2/10/64, 1/12/64	25/2/64, 25/4/64, 24/6/64, 23/8/64, 22/10/64, 21/12/64	26/1/64, 26/3/64, 25/5/64, 24/7/64, 22/9/64, 21/11/64	15/2/64, 15/4/64, 14/6/64, 13/8/64, 12/10/64, 11/12/64	6/1/64, 6/3/64, 5/5/64, 4/7/64, 2/9/64, 1/11/64, 31/12/64

70	13/2/70, 14/4/70, 13/6/70, 12/8/70, 11/10/70, 10/12/70	4/1/70, 5/3/70, 4/5/70, 3/7/70, 1/9/70, 31/10/70, 30/12/70	24/1/70, 25/3/70, 24/5/70, 23/7/70, 21/9/70, 20/11/70	23/2/70, 24/4/70, 23/6/70, 22/8/70, 21/10/70, 20/12/70	14/1/70, 15/3/70, 14/5/70, 13/7/70, 11/9/70, 10/11/70	3/2/70, 4/4/70, 3/6/70, 2/8/70, 1/10/70, 30/11/70
71	8/2/71, 9/4/71, 8/6/71, 7/8/71, 6/10/71, 5/12/71	28/2/71, 29/4/71, 28/6/71, 27/8/71, 26/10/71, 25/12/71	19/1/71, 20/3/71, 19/5/71, 18/7/71, 16/9/71, 15/11/71	18/2/71, 19/4/71, 18/6/71, 17/8/71, 16/10/71, 15/12/71	9/1/71, 10/3/71, 9/5/71, 8/7/71, 6/9/71, 5/11/71	29/1/71, 30/3/71, 29/5/71, 28/7/71, 26/9/71, 25/11/71
72	3/2/72, 3/4/72, 2/6/72, 1/8/72, 30/9/72, 29/11/72	23/2/72, 23/4/72, 22/6/72, 21/8/72, 20/10/72, 19/12/72	14/1/72, 14/3/72, 13/5/72, 12/7/72, 10/9/72, 9/11/72	13/2/72, 13/4/72, 12/6/72, 11/8/72, 10/10/72, 9/12/72	4/1/72, 4/3/72, 3/5/72, 2/7/72, 31/8/72, 30/10/72, 29/12/72	24/1/72, 24/3/72, 23/5/72, 22/7/72, 20/9/72, 19/11/72
73	28/1/73, 29/3/73, 28/5/73, 27/7/73, 25/9/73, 24/11/73	17/2/73, 18/4/73, 17/6/73, 16/8/73, 15/10/73, 14/12/73	8/1/73, 9/3/73, 8/5/73, 7/7/73, 5/9/73, 4/11/73	7/2/73, 8/4/73, 7/6/73, 6/8/73, 5/10/73, 4/12/73	27/2/73, 28/4/73, 27/6/73, 26/8/73, 25/10/73, 24/12/73	18/1/73, 19/3/73, 18/5/73, 17/7/73, 15/9/73, 14/11/73
74	23/1/74, 24/3/74, 23/5/74, 22/7/74, 20/9/74, 19/11/74	12/2/74, 13/4/74, 12/6/74, 11/8/74, 10/10/74, 9/12/74	3/1/74, 4/3/74, 3/5/74, 2/7/74, 31/8/74, 30/10/74, 29/12/74	2/2/74, 3/4/74, 2/6/74, 1/8/74, 30/9/74, 29/11/74	22/2/74, 23/4/74, 22/6/74, 21/8/74, 20/10/74, 19/12/74	13/1/74, 14/3/74, 13/5/74, 12/7/74, 10/9/74, 9/11/74

80	21/2/80, 21/4/80, 20/6/80, 19/8/80, 18/10/80, 17/12/80	12/1/80, 12/3/80, 11/5/80, 10/7/80, 8/9/80, 7/11/80	1/2/80, 1/4/80, 31/5/80, 30/7/80, 28/9/80, 27/11/80	2/1/80, 2/3/80, 1/5/80, 30/6/80, 29/8/80, 28/10/80, 27/12/80	22/1/80, 22/3/80, 21/5/80, 20/7/80, 18/9/80, 17/11/80	11/2/80, 11/4/80, 10/6/80, 9/8/80, 8/10/80, 7/12/80
81	15/2/81, 16/4/81, 15/6/81, 14/8/81, 13/10/81, 12/12/81	6/1/81, 7/3/81, 6/5/81, 5/7/81, 3/9/81, 2/11/81	26/1/81, 27/3/81, 26/5/81, 25/7/81, 23/9/81, 22/11/81	25/2/81, 26/4/81, 25/6/81, 24/8/81, 23/10/81, 22/12/81	16/1/81, 17/3/81, 16/5/81, 15/7/81, 13/9/81, 12/11/81	5/2/81, 6/4/81, 5/6/81, 4/8/81, 3/10/81, 2/12/81
82	10/2/82, 11/4/82, 10/6/82, 9/8/82, 8/10/82, 7/12/82	1/1/82, 2/3/82, 1/5/82, 30/6/82, 29/8/82, 28/10/82, 27/12/82	21/1/82, 22/3/82, 21/5/82, 20/7/82, 18/9/82, 17/11/82	20/2/82, 21/4/82, 20/6/82, 19/8/82, 18/10/82, 17/12/82	11/1/82, 12/3/82, 11/5/82, 10/7/82, 8/9/82, 7/11/82	31/1/82, 1/4/82, 31/5/82, 30/7/82, 28/9/82, 27/11/82
83	5/2/83, 6/4/83, 5/6/83, 4/8/83, 3/10/83, 2/12/83	25/2/83, 26/4/83, 25/6/83, 24/8/83, 23/10/83, 22/12/83	16/1/83, 17/3/83, 16/5/83, 15/7/83, 13/9/83, 12/11/83	15/2/83, 16/4/83, 15/6/83, 14/8/83, 13/10/83, 12/12/83	6/1/83, 7/3/83, 6/5/83, 5/7/83, 3/9/83, 2/11/83	26/1/83, 27/3/83, 26/5/83, 25/7/83, 23/9/83, 22/11/83
84	31/1/84, 31/3/84, 30/5/84, 29/7/84, 27/9/84, 26/11/84	20/2/84, 20/4/84, 19/6/84, 18/8/84, 17/10/84, 16/12/84	11/1/84, 11/3/84, 10/5/84, 9/7/84, 7/9/84, 6/11/84	10/2/84, 10/4/84, 9/6/84, 8/8/84, 7/10/84, 6/12/84	1/1/84, 1/3/84, 30/4/84, 29/6/84, 28/8/84, 27/10/84, 26/12/84	21/1/84, 21/3/84, 20/5/84, 19/7/84, 17/9/84, 16/11/84

90	28/2/90, 29/4/90, 28/6/90, 27/8/90, 26/10/90, 25/12/90	19/1/90, 20/3/90, 19/5/90, 18/7/90, 16/9/90, 15/11/90	8/2/90, 9/4/90, 8/6/90, 7/8/90, 6/10/90, 5/12/90	9/1/90, 10/3/90, 9/5/90, 8/7/90, 6/9/90, 5/11/90	29/1/90, 30/3/90, 29/5/90, 28/7/90, 26/9/90, 25/11/90	18/2/90, 19/4/90, 18/6/90, 17/8/90, 16/10/90, 15/12/90
91	23/2/91, 24/4/91, 23/6/91, 22/8/91, 21/10/91, 20/12/91	14/1/91, 15/3/91, 14/5/91, 13/7/91, 11/9/91, 10/11/91	3/2/91, 4/4/91, 3/6/91, 2/8/91, 1/10/91, 30/11/91	4/1/91, 5/3/91, 4/5/91, 3/7/91, 1/9/91, 31/10/91, 30/12/91	24/1/91, 25/3/91, 24/5/91, 23/7/91, 21/9/91, 20/11/91	13/2/91, 14/4/91, 13/6/91, 12/8/91, 11/10/91, 10/12/91
92	18/2/92, 18/4/92, 17/6/92, 16/8/92, 15/10/92, 14/12/92	9/1/92, 9/3/92, 8/5/92, 7/7/92, 5/9/92, 4/11/92	29/1/92, 29/3/92, 28/5/92, 27/7/92, 25/9/92, 24/11/92	28/2/92, 28/4/92, 27/6/92, 26/8/92, 25/10/92, 24/12/92	19/1/92, 19/3/92, 18/5/92, 17/7/92, 15/9/92, 14/11/92	8/2/92, 8/4/92, 7/6/92, 6/8/92, 5/10/92, 4/12/92
93	12/2/93, 13/4/93, 12/6/93, 11/8/93, 10/10/93, 9/12/93	3/1/93, 4/3/93, 3/5/93, 2/7/93, 31/8/93, 30/10/93, 29/12/93	23/1/93, 24/3/93, 23/5/93, 22/7/93, 20/9/93, 19/11/93	22/2/93, 23/4/93, 22/6/93, 21/8/93, 20/10/93, 19/12/93	13/1/93, 14/3/93, 13/5/93, 12/7/93, 10/9/93, 9/11/93	2/2/93, 3/4/93, 2/6/93, 1/8/93, 30/9/93, 29/11/93
94	7/2/94, 8/4/94, 7/6/94, 6/8/94, 5/10/94, 4/12/94	27/2/94, 28/4/94, 27/6/94, 26/8/94, 25/10/94, 24/12/94	18/1/94, 19/3/94, 18/5/94, 17/7/94, 15/9/94, 14/11/94	17/2/94, 18/4/94, 17/6/94, 16/8/94, 15/10/94, 14/12/94	8/1/94, 9/3/94, 8/5/94, 7/7/94, 5/9/94, 4/11/94	28/1/94, 29/3/94, 28/5/94, 27/7/94, 25/9/94, 24/11/94

dragon & snake | tiger & rabbit | rat & ox

45

24/2/45	15/1/45	4/2/45
25/4/45	16/3/45	5/4/45
24/6/45	15/5/45	4/6/45
23/8/45	14/7/45	3/8/45
22/10/45	12/9/45	2/10/45
21/12/45	11/11/45	1/12/45

5/1/45	25/1/45	14/2/45
6/3/45	26/3/45	15/4/45
5/5/45	25/5/45	14/6/45
4/7/45	24/7/45	13/8/45
2/9/45	22/9/45	12/10/45
1/11/45	21/11/45	11/12/45
31/12/45		

46

19/2/46	10/1/46	30/1/46
20/4/46	11/3/46	31/3/46
19/6/46	10/5/46	30/5/46
18/8/46	9/7/46	29/7/46
17/10/46	7/9/46	27/9/46
16/12/46	6/11/46	26/11/46

1/3/46	20/1/46	9/2/46
30/4/46	21/3/46	10/4/46
29/6/46	20/5/46	9/6/46
28/8/46	19/7/46	8/8/46
27/10/46	17/9/46	7/10/46
26/12/46	16/11/46	6/12/46

47

14/2/47	5/1/47	25/1/47
15/4/47	6/3/47	26/3/47
14/6/47	5/5/47	25/5/47
13/8/47	4/7/47	24/7/47
12/10/47	2/9/47	22/9/47
11/12/47	1/11/47	21/11/47
	31/12/47	

24/2/47	15/1/47	4/2/47
25/4/47	16/3/47	5/4/47
24/6/47	15/5/47	4/6/47
23/8/47	14/7/47	3/8/47
22/10/47	12/9/47	2/10/47
21/12/47	11/11/47	1/12/47

48

9/2/48	29/2/48	20/1/48
9/4/48	29/4/48	20/3/48
8/6/48	28/6/48	19/5/48
7/8/48	27/8/48	18/7/48
6/10/48	26/10/48	16/9/48
5/12/48	25/12/48	15/11/48

19/2/48	10/1/48	30/1/48
19/4/48	10/3/48	30/3/48
18/6/48	9/5/48	29/5/48
17/8/48	8/7/48	28/7/48
16/10/48	6/9/48	26/9/48
15/12/48	5/11/48	25/11/48

49

3/2/49	23/2/49	14/1/49
4/4/49	24/4/49	15/3/49
3/6/49	23/6/49	14/5/49
2/8/49	22/8/49	13/7/49
1/10/49	21/10/49	11/9/49
30/11/49	20/12/49	10/11/49

13/2/49	4/1/49	24/1/49
14/4/49	5/3/49	25/3/49
13/6/49	4/5/49	24/5/49
12/8/49	3/7/49	23/7/49
11/10/49	1/9/49	21/9/49
10/12/49	31/10/49	20/11/49
	30/12/49	

55

3/1/55	23/1/55	12/2/55
4/3/55	24/3/55	13/4/55
3/5/55	23/5/55	12/6/55
2/7/55	22/7/55	11/8/55
31/8/55	20/9/55	10/10/55
30/10/55	19/11/55	9/12/55
29/12/55		

13/1/55	2/2/55	22/2/55
14/3/55	3/4/55	23/4/55
13/5/55	2/6/55	22/6/55
12/7/55	1/8/55	21/8/55
10/9/55	30/9/55	20/10/55
9/11/55	29/11/55	19/12/55

56

27/2/56	18/1/56	7/2/56
27/4/56	18/3/56	7/4/56
26/6/56	17/5/56	6/6/56
25/8/56	16/7/56	5/8/56
24/10/56	14/9/56	4/10/56
23/12/56	13/11/56	3/12/56

8/1/56	28/1/56	17/2/56
8/3/56	28/3/56	17/4/56
7/5/56	27/5/56	16/6/56
6/7/56	26/7/56	15/8/56
4/9/56	24/9/56	14/10/56
3/11/56	23/11/56	13/12/56

57

21/2/57	12/1/57	1/2/57
22/4/57	13/3/57	2/4/57
21/6/57	12/5/57	1/6/57
20/8/57	11/7/57	31/7/57
19/10/57	9/9/57	29/9/57
18/12/57	8/11/57	28/11/57

2/1/57	22/1/57	11/2/57
3/3/57	23/3/57	12/4/57
2/5/57	22/5/57	11/6/57
1/7/57	21/7/57	10/8/57
30/8/57	19/9/57	9/10/57
29/10/57	18/11/57	8/12/57
28/12/57		

58

16/2/58	7/1/58	27/1/58
17/4/58	8/3/58	28/3/58
16/6/58	7/5/58	27/5/58
15/8/58	6/7/58	26/7/58
14/10/58	4/9/58	24/9/58
13/12/58	3/11/58	23/11/58

26/2/58	17/1/58	6/2/58
27/4/58	18/3/58	7/4/58
26/6/58	17/5/58	6/6/58
25/8/58	16/7/58	5/8/58
24/10/58	14/9/58	4/10/58
23/12/58	13/11/58	3/12/58

59

11/2/59	2/1/59	22/1/59
12/4/59	3/3/59	23/3/59
11/6/59	2/5/59	22/5/59
10/8/59	1/7/59	21/7/59
9/10/59	30/8/59	19/9/59
8/12/59	29/10/59	18/11/59
	28/12/59	

21/2/59	12/1/59	1/2/59
22/4/59	13/3/59	2/4/59
21/6/59	12/5/59	1/6/59
20/8/59	11/7/59	31/7/59
19/10/59	9/9/59	29/9/59
18/12/59	8/11/59	28/11/59

65

10/1/65	30/1/65	19/2/65
11/3/65	31/3/65	20/4/65
10/5/65	30/5/65	19/6/65
9/7/65	29/7/65	18/8/65
7/9/65	27/9/65	17/10/65
6/11/65	26/11/65	16/12/65

20/1/65	9/2/65	1/3/65
21/3/65	10/4/65	30/4/65
20/5/65	9/6/65	29/6/65
19/7/65	8/8/65	28/8/65
17/9/65	7/10/65	27/10/65
16/11/65	6/12/65	26/12/65

66

5/1/66	25/1/66	14/2/66
6/3/66	26/3/66	15/4/66
5/5/66	25/5/66	14/6/66
4/7/66	24/7/66	13/8/66
2/9/66	22/9/66	12/10/66
1/11/66	21/11/66	11/12/66
31/12/66		

15/1/66	4/2/66	24/2/66
16/3/66	5/4/66	25/4/66
15/5/66	4/6/66	24/6/66
14/7/66	3/8/66	23/8/66
12/9/66	2/10/66	22/10/66
11/11/66	1/12/66	21/12/66

67

1/3/67	20/1/67	9/2/67
30/4/67	21/3/67	10/4/67
29/6/67	20/5/67	9/6/67
28/8/67	19/7/67	8/8/67
27/10/67	17/9/67	7/10/67
26/12/67	16/11/67	6/12/67

10/1/67	30/1/67	19/2/67
11/3/67	31/3/67	20/4/67
10/5/67	30/5/67	19/6/67
9/7/67	29/7/67	18/8/67
7/9/67	27/9/67	17/10/67
6/11/67	26/11/67	16/12/67

68

24/2/68	15/1/68	4/2/68
24/4/68	15/3/68	4/4/68
23/6/68	14/5/68	3/6/68
22/8/68	13/7/68	2/8/68
21/10/68	11/9/68	1/10/68
20/12/68	10/11/68	30/11/68

5/1/68	25/1/68	14/2/68
5/3/68	25/3/68	14/4/68
4/5/68	24/5/68	13/6/68
3/7/68	23/7/68	12/8/68
1/9/68	21/9/68	11/10/68
31/10/68	20/11/68	10/12/68
30/12/68		

69

18/2/69	9/1/69	29/1/69
19/4/69	10/3/69	30/3/69
18/6/69	9/5/69	29/5/69
17/8/69	8/7/69	28/7/69
16/10/69	6/9/69	26/9/69
15/12/69	5/11/69	25/11/69

28/2/69	19/1/69	8/2/69
29/4/69	20/3/69	9/4/69
28/6/69	19/5/69	8/6/69
27/8/69	18/7/69	7/8/69
26/10/69	16/9/69	6/10/69
25/12/69	15/11/69	5/12/69

75

18/1/75	7/2/75	27/2/75
19/3/75	8/4/75	28/4/75
18/5/75	7/6/75	27/6/75
17/7/75	6/8/75	26/8/75
15/9/75	5/10/75	25/10/75
14/11/75	4/12/75	24/12/75

28/1/75	17/2/75	8/1/75
29/3/75	18/4/75	9/3/75
28/5/75	17/6/75	8/5/75
27/7/75	16/8/75	7/7/75
25/9/75	15/10/75	5/9/75
24/11/75	14/12/75	4/11/75

76

13/1/76	2/2/76	22/2/76
13/3/76	2/4/76	22/4/76
12/5/76	1/6/76	21/6/76
11/7/76	31/7/76	20/8/76
9/9/76	29/9/76	19/10/76
8/11/76	28/11/76	18/12/76

23/1/76	12/2/76	3/1/76
23/3/76	12/4/76	3/3/76
22/5/76	11/6/76	2/5/76
21/7/76	10/8/76	1/7/76
19/9/76	9/10/76	30/8/76
18/11/76	8/12/76	29/10/76
		28/12/76

77

7/1/77	27/1/77	16/2/77
8/3/77	28/3/77	17/4/77
7/5/77	27/5/77	16/6/77
6/7/77	26/7/77	15/8/77
4/9/77	24/9/77	14/10/77
3/11/77	23/11/77	13/12/77

17/1/77	6/2/77	26/2/77
18/3/77	7/4/77	27/4/77
17/5/77	6/6/77	26/6/77
16/7/77	5/8/77	25/8/77
14/9/77	4/10/77	24/10/77
13/11/77	3/12/77	23/12/77

78

2/1/78	22/1/78	11/2/78
3/3/78	23/3/78	12/4/78
2/5/78	22/5/78	11/6/78
1/7/78	21/7/78	10/8/78
30/8/78	19/9/78	9/10/78
29/10/78	18/11/78	8/12/78
28/12/78		

12/1/78	1/2/78	21/2/78
13/3/78	2/4/78	22/4/78
12/5/78	1/6/78	21/6/78
11/7/78	31/7/78	20/8/78
9/9/78	29/9/78	19/10/78
8/11/78	28/11/78	18/12/78

79

26/2/79	17/1/79	6/2/79
27/4/79	18/3/79	7/4/79
26/6/79	17/5/79	6/6/79
25/8/79	16/7/79	5/8/79
24/10/79	14/9/79	4/10/79
23/12/79	13/11/79	3/12/79

7/1/79	27/1/79	16/2/79
8/3/79	28/3/79	17/4/79
7/5/79	27/5/79	16/6/79
6/7/79	26/7/79	15/8/79
4/9/79	24/9/79	14/10/79
3/11/79	23/11/79	13/12/79

85

25/1/85	14/2/85	5/1/85
26/3/85	15/4/85	6/3/85
25/5/85	14/6/85	5/5/85
24/7/85	13/8/85	4/7/85
22/9/85	12/10/85	2/9/85
21/11/85	11/12/85	1/11/85
		31/12/85

4/2/85	24/2/85	15/1/85
5/4/85	25/4/85	16/3/85
4/6/85	24/6/85	15/5/85
3/8/85	23/8/85	14/7/85
2/10/85	22/10/85	12/9/85
1/12/85	21/12/85	11/11/85

86

20/1/86	9/2/86	1/3/86
21/3/86	10/4/86	30/4/86
20/5/86	9/6/86	29/6/86
19/7/86	8/8/86	28/8/86
17/9/86	7/10/86	27/10/86
16/11/86	6/12/86	26/12/86

30/1/86	19/2/86	10/1/86
31/3/86	20/4/86	11/3/86
30/5/86	19/6/86	10/5/86
29/7/86	18/8/86	9/7/86
27/9/86	17/10/86	7/9/86
26/11/86	16/12/86	6/11/86

87

15/1/87	4/2/87	24/2/87
16/3/87	5/4/87	25/4/87
15/5/87	4/6/87	24/6/87
14/7/87	3/8/87	23/8/87
12/9/87	2/10/87	22/10/87
11/11/87	1/12/87	21/12/87

25/1/87	14/2/87	5/1/87
26/3/87	15/4/87	6/3/87
25/5/87	14/6/87	5/5/87
24/7/87	13/8/87	4/7/87
22/9/87	12/10/87	2/9/87
21/11/87	11/12/87	1/11/87
		31/12/87

88

10/1/88	30/1/88	19/2/88
10/3/88	30/3/88	19/4/88
9/5/88	29/5/88	18/6/88
8/7/88	28/7/88	17/8/88
6/9/88	26/9/88	16/10/88
5/11/88	25/11/88	15/12/88

20/1/88	9/2/88	29/2/88
20/3/88	9/4/88	29/4/88
19/5/88	8/6/88	28/6/88
18/7/88	7/8/88	27/8/88
16/9/88	6/10/88	26/10/88
15/11/88	5/12/88	25/12/88

89

4/1/89	24/1/89	13/2/89
5/3/89	25/3/89	14/4/89
4/5/89	24/5/89	13/6/89
3/7/89	23/7/89	12/8/89
1/9/89	21/9/89	11/10/89
31/10/89	20/11/89	10/12/89
30/12/89		

14/1/89	3/2/89	23/2/89
15/3/89	4/4/89	24/4/89
14/5/89	3/6/89	23/6/89
13/7/89	2/8/89	22/8/89
11/9/89	1/10/89	21/10/89
10/11/89	30/11/89	20/12/89

95

2/2/95	22/2/95	13/1/95
3/4/95	23/4/95	14/3/95
2/6/95	22/6/95	13/5/95
1/8/95	21/8/95	12/7/95
30/9/95	20/10/95	10/9/95
29/11/95	19/12/95	9/11/95

12/2/95	3/1/95	23/1/95
13/4/95	4/3/95	24/3/95
12/6/95	3/5/95	23/5/95
11/8/95	2/7/95	22/7/95
10/10/95	31/8/95	20/9/95
9/12/95	30/10/95	19/11/95
	29/12/95	

96

28/1/96	17/2/96	8/1/96
28/3/96	17/4/96	8/3/96
27/5/96	16/6/96	7/5/96
26/7/96	15/8/96	6/7/96
24/9/96	14/10/96	4/9/96
23/11/96	13/12/96	3/11/96

7/2/96	27/2/96	18/1/96
7/4/96	27/4/96	18/3/96
6/6/96	26/6/96	17/5/96
5/8/96	25/8/96	16/7/96
4/10/96	24/10/96	14/9/96
3/12/96	23/12/96	13/11/96

97

22/1/97	11/2/97	2/1/97
23/3/97	12/4/97	3/3/97
22/5/97	11/6/97	2/5/97
21/7/97	10/8/97	1/7/97
19/9/97	9/10/97	30/8/97
18/11/97	8/12/97	29/10/97
		28/12/97

1/2/97	21/2/97	12/1/97
2/4/97	22/4/97	13/3/97
1/6/97	21/6/97	12/5/97
31/7/97	20/8/97	11/7/97
29/9/97	19/10/97	9/9/97
28/11/97	18/12/97	8/11/97

98

17/1/98	6/2/98	26/2/98
18/3/98	7/4/98	27/4/98
17/5/98	6/6/98	26/6/98
16/7/98	5/8/98	25/8/98
14/9/98	4/10/98	24/10/98
13/11/98	3/12/98	23/12/98

27/1/98	16/2/98	7/1/98
28/3/98	17/4/98	8/3/98
27/5/98	16/6/98	7/5/98
26/7/98	15/8/98	6/7/98
24/9/98	14/10/98	4/9/98
23/11/98	13/12/98	3/11/98

99

12/1/99	1/2/99	21/2/99
13/3/99	2/4/99	22/4/99
12/5/99	1/6/99	21/6/99
11/7/99	31/7/99	20/8/99
9/9/99	29/9/99	19/10/99
8/11/99	28/11/99	18/12/99

22/1/99	11/2/99	2/1/99
23/3/99	12/4/99	3/3/99
22/5/99	11/6/99	2/5/99
21/7/99	10/8/99	1/7/99
19/9/99	9/10/99	30/8/99
18/11/99	8/12/99	29/10/99

moves

The timing and direction of a move can have a major impact on your ki energy. This is because your personal ki energy mixes more positively with the ki energies associated with some directions than it does with others. And because the pattern of ki changes from one year to the next, the directions that are favourable to you will also change. By moving in a favourable or supportive direction, you may find it easier to make the most of your personal ki energy, whereas moving in a direction with a more destructive ki energy can cause a negative effect.

To help you understand how this process works, imagine moving a plant. First of all, you would take the plant out of its existing soil in a way that does not harm it. Then you would replant it at a time of year that encourages it to become established in its new environment. Finally, you would make sure it was planted in the kind of soil that encourages it to grow well. If all these stages are beneficial for the plant, it will thrive in its new location and could grow even more quickly than before. We are just the same: wherever we live, our ki energy mixes with the ki energy of the local environment in the same way that a plant's roots learn how to live in its surrounding soil. When you leave one place it is almost as though you literally pull your roots out of the soil – you pull your personal ki energy out of the local ki energy to which you have become accustomed.

Moves to encourage your aims

The interaction of different types of ki energies has the biggest effect when you are moving house. However, the interaction of personal and local ki energy can also influence the outcome of other types of moves, such as a new job or any type of travel, whether it be business-related or for pleasure. The local ki energy influences the movement of our own ki energy, which in turn influences our thoughts, emotions and ideas. Every country and large city has pockets that tend to support certain activities. Artists, writers, bankers, musicians, advertising companies, PR companies, actors and wealthy merchants often gravitate to particular areas where they feel the local ki energy is supportive to whatever it is that they are doing.

When moving to a new home or work place, you have the opportunity to enhance your life so you flourish in the same way as a healthy plant. Conversely, moving in a direction and at a time that does not suit

Living in good ki energy

The direction of your new house in relation to your old one contributes to the ki energy you experience once you move there, but you can also create good ki energy by decorating with suitable yin or yang colours (see page 75).

your own ki energy is more likely to cause you to wither, just like a seed planted in the wrong season. The feng shui secret to fulfilling the dreams you hold for the future is to plant these dreams at a time and in a place where they can flower into reality.

The same principle applies to renovations. As you change your home or work space you alter the ki energy in that part of the building. If the direction in which the change happens is favourable for you at the time, the result will be positive with a harmonious mixture of ki energy. But if it involves a direction where the ki energy is not harmonious with your personal ki energy at the time, you may run into unexpected difficulties.

Determining directions

To identify which direction will contribute to a favourable move for you, take a look at the chart on the following page. The most auspicious directions for you each year are indicated wherever you see the colour associated with your nine ki year number. Don't forget that the nine ki year always begins in February, so if you are intending to move prior to the 4th or 5th of February, look at the year before. For example, if you have a nine ki year number five and plan to move after 19.39 GMT on 4 February 2000, the most favourable directions in which you can move that year are south-east, south-west and west.

Next, take a map showing the area you live in and the areas to which you are considering moving. Mark your current home with an X. Draw a line from your home going due north. True north, towards the top of the map is acceptable. Then, using the compass on page 12 as a reference, draw or trace the eight directions so that the centre of the compass is over your home and the north of the compass is aligned with the north on your map (see right). This shows you which areas are located in the most beneficial directions for your new home or workplace.

If you are trying to decide on a holiday destination or the best time for a business trip abroad, substitute your local map for a world map. I use a Peters' projection, which shows geographical points in a more precise directional relationship than other projections. When deciding on the timing of an intended trip, bear in mind that the time you leave your home is more important than the time of your bus, train or flight.

Favourable directions

Each direction you move into has a certain type of ki energy that influences your personal ki energy. Moving north at a favourable time, for example, will ensure that you are more successful at establishing independence and achieving your artistic goals. Moving south at a favourable time helps to raise your public profile and win awards.

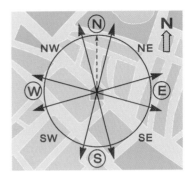

Which way?
Trace the feng shui compass from page 12 over a map of your current home, making sure to align the north of the eight directions with true north on your map. Then use the chart on page 120 to determine which directions from your home are favourable each year.

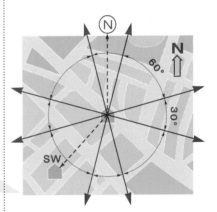

If you are planning to move
To find out if a proposed house move is going to be propitious for you, draw the eight directions with their 30° and 60° segments on a map large enough to show both buildings, with the centre over your existing home. Note the direction in which your intended home lies and then check on page 120 that this is a beneficial direction for you.

favourable directions for moving

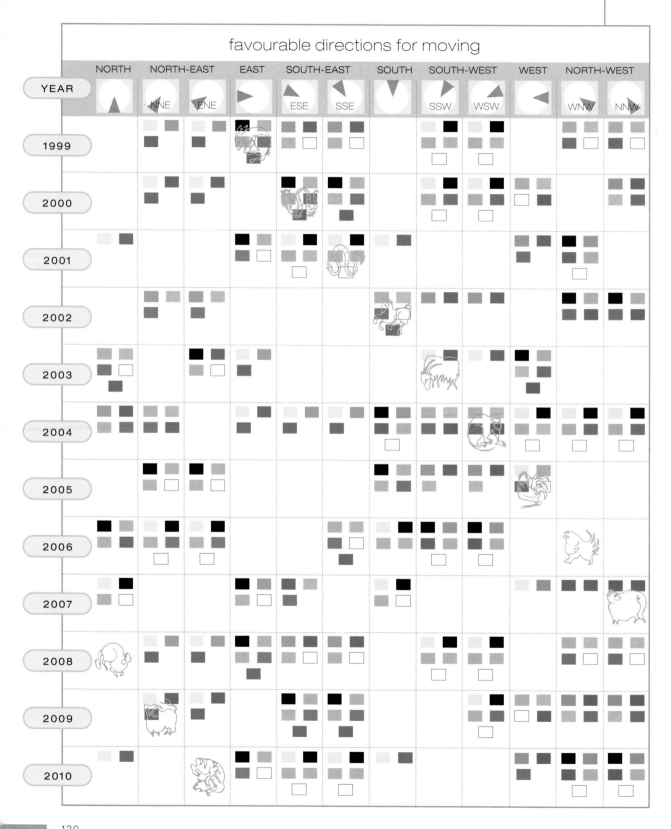

Nine ki years and colours

Every nine ki year number relates to a colour, shown right. If your colour is listed under one of the directions in the chart on the left, this direction is considered a favourable move for you.

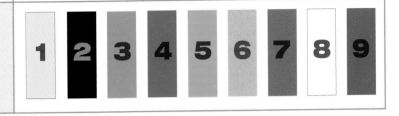

When you travel, you move not only into the ki energy of a particular direction, but also into the ki energy of a particular number. (An exception to this is during years when the number five is at the centre of the year chart. At these times the ki energy of the direction and the number will be the same. See also page 123.) If you move south-east in the year 2000, for example, you will be moving not only into the ki energy of the south-east, but also into the ki energy associated with eight, making you feel more creative and motivated. The chart on page 122 lists the benefits you could hope for when moving in each of the eight directions. These should be considered in conjunction with the ki energy of the number that is in each direction (see pages 72–93). Remember, to experience any of the benefits you need to move in a direction that is favourable for your year number in the year that you are moving.

Harmful directions

Every year, there are some directions that are unfavourable for everyone. You will see on the chart opposite, for example, that nobody is advised to move north, south or west in 2000. But before making a final decision, bear in mind that there are seven additional types of moves that can be potentially harmful, as listed below in order of importance. The first four have the potential to cause the greatest harm: travelling towards or away from five or your own nine ki year number may begin a process that gets worse over the years. The last three are less harmful: travelling away from the most active animal that year, towards a number opposite its normal position or into a five element that is not harmonious to your nine ki year number will begin a process that will fade away. To do this, write out the appropriate chart of the year or month you are planning to move (see page 108) and assess the following:

Moving towards five Beware of moving in a direction that takes you towards the number five in the nine ki chart of any year. In the year 2000, for example, five is in the north. Moving north in this year is considered dangerous because five is the most powerful energy and can lead to unpredictable results and stress, causing the gradual deterioration of your health, business or career.

favourable moves

1 · north

Travelling north, which is associated with the number one, will help you feel more independent, objective and at peace. The north is generally favourable for privacy, making it a good direction to move into if you are keen to hide away or seek seclusion – for a secret sexual encounter, for example. It could be useful if you want to find a place to write, paint or do something artistic. Can also aid convalescence and healing.

8 · north-east

Moving north-east, or into the ki energy of the number eight, is useful if you would like to feel more motivated or gain a clearer sense of the direction you should take in your life. Such a move would be helpful if you felt stuck in a rut and needed a change as it encourages clear-mindedness. It could also help you focus on managing affairs to your own benefit rather than feeling you always need to worry about other people.

3 · east

The ki energy of the east is also associated with the number three. East is a good direction to travel in if you would like to be more ambitious, confident or enthusiastic. Moving in this direction also helps you to feel more active and better able to build up your life. From a business perspective, it is an auspicious direction in which to start a new business or job – or to aid a company's expansion.

4 · south-east

A move south-east, or into the ki energy of the number four, will fire your imagination and encourage creativity. The south-east would be conducive to working on a film, book or piece of music, for instance. It would also help you feel more persistent and tenacious. It is a good direction to go to start a relationship or to get married. Equally it would be a supportive one for starting a new career, job or business.

9 · south

Moving south, which is associated with the number nine, you are likely to feel more emotional, passionate and fiery. It would be useful to go in this direction if you want be noticed, win awards or raise your public profile. It also would help you express yourself, making it beneficial for acting and drama. This would be a good direction to meet new friends and build up an active social life.

2 · south-west

South-westerly travel is recommended for seeking a more practical and down-to-earth approach to life. Also related to the ki energy of the number two, the southwest is good for team working, developing long-term friendships and making steady progress. It can help you consolidate your achievements, develop harmonious relationships with your family and concentrate on improving your quality of life.

7 · west

A move west, or towards the ki energy of number seven, will help you feel more content and better able to enjoy the pleasures in life. The west is associated with romance, so it is a helpful direction in which to start a relationship or get married. It could also help you focus more on ways to increase your financial income, so consider moving west to arrange financial backing or a loan, get a new job or start a business.

6 · north-west

The north-west is a useful direction if you would like to be more in control of your life. It can make you feel dignified, graceful and authoritative. A move in this direction, or towards the number 6, would make it easier to command respect and be seen as someone with honour and integrity. So if you are hoping for a promotion, applying for a new leadership position or taking on greater responsibilities, aim north-west.

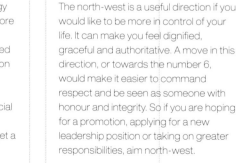

Moving away from five This is considered dangerous because you are moving away from a potentially destructive force, which can weaken your own personal ki energy and make you more more vulnerable to accidents, injuries and robberies. You may feel as though you are in a vacuum with less energy than usual.

Moving towards your year number Travelling into your own ki energy is like pushing two magnets together. By forcing your own ki energy into a direction that already has the same ki energy, you can become confused and unsettled, making it hard to be decisive or clear minded. Simple events can also turn out unnecessarily complicated.

Moving away from your year number Travelling away from your nine ki year number in any year is like leaving a part of you behind and can result in a loss of confidence. You may feel empty and be unable to organise your life properly. If your own nine ki year number is five, moving towards or away from the ki energy of five in a particular year is also the same as moving to or from your own nine ki year number, and this increases the risk of your ki energy being harmed.

Moving away from the animal of the year Every year is related to one of the 12 astrological animals and each year the direction associated with that animal develops more active ki energy. Travelling in a direction that takes you away from the ki energy of the animal of that year can lead to a deficiency in your own ki energy and, in particular, situations breaking up. This could be the destruction of a relationship, separation from your family or disruption to business negotiations or contracts. For example, 2000 is the year of the dragon, which is associated with the east-south-east. In the year 2000 anyone, regardless of his or her year number, who moves away from this direction (that is, moves west-north-west) will be risking weakened personal ki energy and disruption.

Moving towards a number opposite its normal position This can cause events to go awry. For example, in the year 2000, seven is to the east. In the standard chart of the magic square, seven is to the west, so in the year 2000 seven is opposite its normal position. So anyone moving east in the year 2000 would ideally keep his or her options open and make alternative arrangements should things not work out as planned.

Moving towards a disharmonious element Your nine ki year number is associated with one of the five elements (see page 10). If you move in a direction that has an element which is not in harmony with

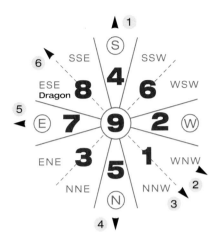

1 Moving away from five

2 Moving away from animal of the year

3 Moving towards year number

4 Moving towards five

5 Moving towards number opposite its normal position

6 Moving away from year number

Plotting the harmful directions

The example above shows how someone with the year number one could work out the inauspicious directions to move in for the year 2000. The most beneficial directions will be north-east and south-west.

the element of your year number, it can create turbulent ki energy. For example, if you have the nine ki year number one, the element related to your year number is water. If you move towards numbers in a year chart that have fire or soil elements, such as two, five, eight and nine, your personal ki energy will be mixing with surrounding ki energy that has disharmonious elements.

Solving bad moves

If, after reading this book, you discover that your new home is in an unfavourable direction for you, don't despair as there are several ways to reorientate your ki energy. For example, if you have recently moved towards or away from the direction of the nine ki number five or your own nine ki year number, you can move temporarily in a beneficial direction, sleep there every night for three months (which is long enough to establish your ki energy there), then return to your permanent home in a favourable direction. If you move to another continent temporarily to reorientate your ki energy, sleeping there every night for two months is sufficient. Ideally, during your time away you would sleep in the same location every night. An example of reorienting your ki energy is if you have the nine ki year number one and it is the year 2000 (when nine is the central number of the chart). South-west or north-east are both favourable directions for you so you should move temporarily in one of these directions. Remember, it is not the route you use to get to a new location (temporary or permanent) but where you were originally and where your final destination is that should be considered when calculating if a move is favourable or not. Also, the greater the distance you move, the stronger and quicker the effects.

Another potential solution if you have moved in an unfavourable direction – though probably not an option for everyone – is to travel all the way around the world in a favourable direction. On returning, you would need to sleep in your home every night for two months before travelling again. For example, in the year 2001 when eight is the central number, someone with the year number seven could travel favourably around the world in an eastern direction. To make this and my previous suggestion worthwhile, you should also find the best months and days to travel. This applies only when you can travel east or west.

If neither of these remedies are practical for you, the next-best solution is to make sure that the first journey you make each day is in a favourable direction for you. If you have the nine ki year number three, for example, and it is the year 2007 (when two is the central number) you should travel daily from your home to a destination in the east. Ideally, you should spend twenty minutes in the favourable direction before moving on, so if this first journey takes you away from your main destination of the day (your office, for example), consider taking a walk to a local park or having an early morning coffee at a cafe that is situated in the correct direction before heading off for work.

Making changes to your home

Whether you are planning to build an extension, convert a loft, carry out renovations or simply redecorate a room, the principles of timing events and moving in a beneficial direction can also be applied when starting these projects. The aim is to alter the flow of ki energy in a part of your home at a time that will be advantageous for you. For instance, if you were to move your bed so that it faced a more favourable direction, it would be advisable to do this

at a time when the ki energy of the new direction is favourable for you. When you change something in your home it has a similar effect to planting a new seed. When you first place a seed in the soil, the first few days are highly influential. Similarly, when you move your bed, the ki energy when you first do this is most important in terms of your ability to thrive. Once you have established yourself in the new direction, the effect of the changes in the flow of ki energy becomes less important.

Often, making changes to your house or apartment will not only affect your home-life but can influence your professional success as well. Adding a water feature such as a fountain to the eastern part of your home, for example, will help build up ki energy associated with your career. To enhance the benefits of this water feature even further, you should install it in the east at a time when the ki energy of the water will grow and develop.

To find favourable times to make changes to your home, locate the chart for the year or month concerned (see page 108). Write the numbers of that year onto your compass of the eight directions. Highlight the whole axis with the number five and your own year number. If other people live with you, highlight their numbers as well. If you are a family consider only the parents' year numbers or the main wage earner's. Reproduce the compass on a plan of your home, making sure that the northern direction lines up with north on your plan. Check which parts of your home are covered by the axis containing five and your year number, and avoid making any significant changes to these areas. This aspect of feng shui astrology can also be used to predict the areas of your home most likely to have problems in a given year, month or day. If foreseen, you can use feng shui solutions to prevent them from occurring.

Establishing new ki energy

Just as a seed will not grow in new soil if it keeps getting moved, you also need time to establish yourself in your new ki energy. If you are moving within the same continent, you need to sleep in the new location every night for at least three months. If it is a different continent you need to sleep there every night for two months.

Index

Acknowledgements

Carroll and Brown would like to thank the following:

Design concept Simon Daley
Design assistance Gilda Pacitti, Dorian Cassidy, Vimit Punater, Adelle Morris
Editorial assistance Dawn Henderson, Nikki Taylor, Caroline Uzielli
Production Wendy Lawson
Computer management John Clifford, Paul Stradling, Elisa Merino
Picture research Richard Soar
Index Madeline Weston

Photographic sources

p. 5 Telegraph Colour Library (bottom); p. 6 Goddard Space Flight Centre/Nasa; p. 7 Carroll & Brown Ltd (bottom); p. 8 The Kobal Collection; p. 9 Telegraph Colour Library; p. 12 Telegraph Colour Library; p. 14 Telegraph Colour Library (top), Carroll & Brown Ltd (bottom); p. 16 Telegraph Colour Library; p. 18 Telegraph Colour Library; p. 25 Rex Features (top), Carroll & Brown Ltd (bottom); p. 26 Rex Features (bottom); p. 27 Rex Features (top), Jules Selmes (bottom); p. 28 The Kobal Collection (top); p. 29 Rex Features (bottom); p. 30 Rex Features (top); p. 31 The Kobal Collection (top); p. 32 Rex Features; p. 33 Rex Features (top); p. 74 Telegraph Colour Library; p. 76 David Murray (right); p. 77 Jules Selmes (left); p. 78 Jules Selmes (right); p. 80 Jules Selmes (right); p. 83 Jules Selmes (left); p. 84 Steven Graham (right); p. 85 Jules Selmes (left); p. 86 David Murray (right); p. 87 Jules Selmes (left); p. 88 Jules Selmes (right); p. 89 Telegraph Colour Library (right); p. 90 Jules Selmes (right); p. 91 Jules Selmes (left); p. 93 Jules Selmes (left); p. 95 Telegraph Colour Library (right); p. 109 Telegraph Colour Library; p. 110 Telegraph Colour Library; p. 118 Telegraph Colour Library; p. 125 Telegraph Colour Library; COVER: Telegraph Colour Library (middle left, middle right), Jules Selmes (bottom left), Carroll & Brown Ltd (bottom centre)

It would have been impossible to have written this book without all the people who I have been able to provide nine ki advice to. My computer is full of names and nine ki code numbers, and all my family and friends have been willing participants in my quest to build up real-life experience with nine ki astrology. I wish to thank you all for making this book possible. I would particularly like to thank my mother, Patsy, Dragana, the woman I adore who has been invaluable with her extraordinary ability to memorise so many people's nine ki numbers, my children Christopher, Alexander, Nicholas and Michael; my brother Adam, Angela and their children; and the Waxmans, especially Melanie and Denny. An enormous thank you to Boy George for all his help over the years, along with Tony Gordon, Tony Denton and Virgin who have had to put up with all my changes to George's travel schedules. Thanks also to: my friends and clients Jeremy Parkin, Kim Andreolli, Enno and Dusica von Landmann, Michael Maloney, Christopher Foyle, the Mosbachers, Mark and Roslyn Palmer, Diana and Jimmy Hern, Ginie Lyras, David Simmons, Mark Dean, Audrey Pissani Crockford, Jerry Thompson and Lorenzo Poccianti; my teachers and colleagues, especially Michio and Aveline Kushi and Shizuko Yamamoto; Nimita Parmar and Stephen Skinner from *Feng Shui for Modern Living*; Jon Sandifer and everyone at the Feng Shui Society; my colleagues John and Maria Brosnan; and everyone at Carroll & Brown, especially Amy Carroll, Denise Brown and Madeleine Jennings.
SIMON BROWN

About the author

Simon Brown began studies in Oriental medicine in 1981. He was the director of London's East-West Centre for seven years, which ran a wide range of courses in the Oriental healing arts, and has since made feng shui his full-time career. His clients include celebrities such as Boy George and large companies including The Body Shop and British Airways. He has written a weekly column for the *Saturday Express* and numerous articles for *Feng Shui for Modern Living*.

Other books by Simon Brown

The Principles Of Feng Shui
Published by Thorsons, ISBN 0-7225-3347-0
Also available on audiocassette

Practical Feng Shui
Published by Ward Lock, ISBN 0-7063-7634-X

Practical Feng Shui for Business
Published by Ward Lock, ISBN 0-7063-7768-0

Consultations with Simon Brown

Simon Brown works as a full time feng shui consultant and lectures in Europe and the USA. For information on feng shui consultations with Simon, call 0171 431 9897 or write to: Simon Brown, PO Box 10453, London, NW3 4WD.
Simon can be also contacted via e-mail at:
106025.3515@compuserve.com
For information on feng shui and nine ki computer products, visit Simon Brown's web site at http://ourworld.compuserve.com/homepages/simonbrown_fengshui